CAN WE
CHANGE
FOR A
CHANGE?

CAN WE
CHANGE
FOR A
CHANGE?

*100 Winning Tips for
Creating a Lasting Change*

MICHELLE ROZEN, PHD

CONTENTS

INTRODUCTION

At the age of 32, I felt extremely frustrated. I was working at a job that I didn't like. I told my husband that I constantly felt I was wearing shoes that were three sizes too small. My days were spent feeling overworked and unappreciated. I was very jealous of any career woman around me that I felt got the career that she deserved, unlike me, who got stuck in a job that I didn't like.

Back then I had a good friend who was a few years older than me. We both had young kids. We used to meet at the local Starbucks at 7:00 a.m. every Saturday morning, before the kids woke up and the day started. One day, I told her how much I hated my job and my day-to-day life. She looked at me and said: "Then change it. Go to school and change your path."

"I wish I could," I told her while holding back the tears. "My kids are so young and they need me. Adam is in a startup and never home. One day, when the time is right, I'll do exactly that."

She gave me a sharp look and then told me the sentence that has changed my life. "Michelle," she said. "You just don't get it, do you? Your kids will always need you and Adam will always be in a startup. Go and sign up for classes this week, and tell me next Saturday that you have done it."

I looked at her, puzzled. What she had told me had never crossed my mind. I'd never thought of it that way.

I was desperate for a change. I went and signed up for my Master's in Psychology. My son was five. My daughter was one. I worked a full-time job and had a husband who constantly traveled.

I found myself setting alarms for 3:00 a.m. I was working until 6:00 a.m. and then waking up to the baby and starting my day. I worked twice as hard, but my life was suddenly full. I had a challenge. I had content. I felt that I was going somewhere.

When I finished my Master's, I was seven months pregnant with my third child. I remember sitting there in the final exam room, disappointed that it would soon be over.

I had a friend who took some classes with me. She was working toward her PhD in Psychology. She had two kids and was working full time. Every time I asked her how she managed to do it, she told me the same sentence: "If I can do it, so can you."

I decided to take what she said literally. If she could do it, so could I.

And so, seven months pregnant, I started my PhD and gave birth to my daughter Mia in the first semester.

The changes I was fighting for in my life became the topic that I was most interested in when I started doing the research for my PhD. What motivates us to change our lives? What stops us? Why are we so afraid? And what keeps us going through difficulty and challenge?

The PhD was definitely a step up in terms of challenge from my Master's. But, this time I was more prepared. I had a goal. I had a detailed plan. And, I had better tools to help me through my daily challenges.

I still kept setting alarms to 3:00 or 4:00 a.m. My kids and family were still my absolute priority. I remember saying to myself: family first, then work, and then school. I felt that I had it all on track.

Then, in 2008, the economy collapsed. My husband's startup was shut down. Things were getting challenging to a near-breaking point. I went and told my husband that I thought that the most sensible thing for me to do was to take a break.

"I will come back to school later," I told him. "When things get better, and the time is right." He looked at me and said two things that I will thank him for every day for the rest of my life. He said, "Who deserves a PhD more than you?" Then, he said: "Michelle, if you leave now, you will not go back. Stay with the program no matter what and finish your degree." And so I stayed.

A few semesters down the road, I found myself struggling with bills, kids, work, and school. I was trying to keep up with it all. At that time, I had a professor who did not think too highly of me. I don't think he realized the kind of struggle that I was in. I got C's in both of his classes and a nice fancy letter from the university. The letter said that I was on probation unless I repeated a class. I literally sat and cried. It was such an insult to me. I was working so hard to keep it all going. Getting that letter made me feel so bad about myself. It made me feel bad about the whole process.

I went home and told my husband that perhaps I should take a break. He said to me, "Michelle, repeat the class. You won't even remember it later. Swallow your pride and repeat the class." And so I did.

The day I got my PhD was not a day about the academic degree. It's nice to get a PhD. It's nice to get any degree. It was a day, for both of us, about working against all odds. A day of incredible teamwork. It was a day of resilience and persistence above and beyond what I thought I had in me.

To Nili, my friend who gave me the best advice I've ever gotten, thank you. Thanks to your honest advice, I was able to turn my life around. To my husband, Adam, thank you, for teaching me important life lessons on persistence and teamwork. To my kids, Roey, Abby, and Mia, thank you for being born. You are the engine for everything that I do. Life works in mysterious ways.

This journey that I went through in my own life got me so fascinated with purpose and perseverance. With how the mind works when it comes to managing life, rather than being managed by it. This is all I research, write, and talk about. This became my life mission, my passion, and my purpose, and what I share with everyone that I meet, on all platforms.

I ask you today to embrace challenge, to read this book with an open mind and an open heart and let yourself be encouraged. This book contains 100 tips for creating a lasting change in your life, and 100 inspirational quotes on those tips. It was created to serve as a reminder to you that you can do amazing things with your life. You *can* transform your life. You *can* turn your struggles into your power wheel, and you *can* achieve the life that you want for yourself and for your family. Believe me, I did it too.

#1

Find Out What You Really Want

"The great secret of getting what you want from life is to know what you want and believe you can have it."
—NORMAN VINCENT PEALE

We often feel very frustrated with a certain aspect of our lives, and in many cases, with more than one. If you feel that you are not happy with certain things in your life, that sense of being uncomfortable, unhappy, not at ease is actually your best news. Embrace it! This is the first thing that will push you toward change. The more unhappy and uncomfortable you are with something in your life, the more likely you are to change it. Here are three questions to ask yourself:

- What am I unhappy about?
- Why am I unhappy about it?
- On a scale of 0-10, how passionately do I want to change it?

Life is busy and full of distractions. There are so many chores, so many responsibilities, so many things to worry about and take care of, not to mention social media, the news, and just so many distractions all around us. We are so distracted and so overloaded with information and stimulations and just all kinds of distractions that we simply do not get to stop and think—what bothers me? Why does it bother me? What am I looking to change, and why?

What this causes in our lives is a general sense of dissatisfaction on the one hand, and a lack of clarity in terms of what actually bothers us on the other. Many people describe a sense of feeling trapped—trapped in their jobs, trapped in their responsibilities, trapped in their relationships, trapped in their bodies, all kinds of feeling trapped, and that does not sound too good or too happy. In other cases, the word 'trapped' may sound too strong, but people just feel that they could do better, could be more fit, healthier, more organized, more efficient with their time, one could accomplish more, but they are not able to create a plan that will get them there, and their attempts to create improvement fail.

Would you run a company without a daily, weekly, or monthly team meeting? I don't think so. Your life should be run in a similar way. You just cannot go on and on and on without pulling out to the sidelines for a few minutes and having a meeting with yourself.

#2

Turn Your Dream into a Plan

"Everything you want is out there waiting for you to ask. Everything you want also wants you. But you have to take action to get it."
—JULES RENARD

Defining what really matters to us the most and what we are looking to change is the first step toward creating a change, but we now need to move forward into creating an action plan. Without an action plan, any goal is just a dream, and we are not in the dreams business, we are in the change business, looking to create lasting change. Here are the five characteristics of a good action plan to create lasting change—make sure your plan has all of them:

It is clear:

The plan has to be clear in terms of what exactly is going to happen. What are you looking to do that will be different than what you have done before? Keep nothing vague, spell it all out. What exactly are you looking to accomplish? What exactly are you looking to do differently? How exactly is that going to happen?

It is realistic:

Don't just go from being someone who goes to the gym once a month to someone with the schedule of an Olympic champion. Don't overlook your schedule and your life circumstances. Don't overlook your personality, sleep patterns, or work habits. You have done this before. You know what your pitfalls are and where you shine. You *know* who you are and you *know* what works and what doesn't. That knowledge is with you. *You* are the expert of *your* life. Use that knowledge for your benefit when you create your plan. Keep it real with a challenge. That's the rule of thumb.

It is specific:

This one is critical. The more specific the plan is, the more likely it is to succeed. Don't say, "I'll be more organized." Get down to details. How will you be more organized? What is your plan for doing that? Will you use an online calendar? Will you use certain apps? Daily lists to cross out? Notes on the fridge? Don't just say, "I'll work hard to become more fit," or "To increase my income." How will you do that? What is your plan? What will you do? How often? When?

It is aligned with your goals:

Pick no more than three goals. Don't bite off more than you can chew! Change is hard—limit yourself to just a few goals. It is challenging, and you need to stay focused around them. Create a detailed and specific plan for each goal. Make sure that your plan supports the goals that you have defined, and that you are focused and clear about your goals and about how your detailed plan supports them.

It is the right plan for you:

What may work for you may not work for someone else, and what may work for someone else may not work for you. The power is in the details. You are the expert of: you. The details of your plan, that are unique to you and to what works and doesn't work for you, will make all the difference in the world. Do not look left and right—it doesn't matter what other people do and how they got there. What matters is what works for you, in your life, with your personality, with your unique challenges and circumstances. There is no cookie-cutter deal here. You have to build your own plan.

#3

Get Detailed

"You can't just sit there and wait for people to give you that golden dream. You've got to get out there and make it happen for yourself."
—Diana Ross

Because life is full of distractions, and we truly and rightfully get tired, it is so easy to get sidetracked and look for every possible excuse not to follow up on our plan. "Tomorrow" promises are something that we are all guilty of. To prevent that, we have to get detailed with our plan, and research shows us across the board that the more detailed a plan is, the more likely it is to be followed.

Here is what the difference looks like:

Vague plan:
Go to the gym more often.

Semi-vague plan:
Go to the gym 2-3 times a week.

Detailed plan:
Go to the gym on Mondays, Wednesdays, and Fridays, between 6:00-7:00 a.m.

Here is another example:

Vague plan:
Make more money.

Semi-vague plan:
Double my income.

Detailed plan:
Double my income by January, by making three sales calls a day and increasing my network by 50%.

See the difference? A vague plan is more like a wish. It will dwindle with the first distraction. A detailed plan is an action plan, and if you stick to it, your likelihood of succeeding is way higher.

Planning ahead and being detailed when we plan is not just a key to success in business, where we create, adjust, and follow business plans as a first step—it is also the master plan to the success in every aspect of our lives. When you take the time to get detailed with your plan, you are planning success. Success doesn't happen by itself, and hard work and a strong desire to succeed are not enough. Success takes planning. Whether you are a planner or not does not matter. It may impact the way you plan or the style of your planning, as some people get more detailed and specific than others, and that's fine—these are personality and style differences and they are to be expected—but having a detailed plan, to the level that you can handle and then a notch more, is critical, and no success can happen without it.

#4

Stop Doing More of the Same

"Change your life today. Don't gamble on the future, act now, without delay."
—SIMON DE BEAUVIOR

You know those people who stand by the elevator, hit the button, and when the elevator is not coming (yet!) hit the button again, and then again with increased intensity, because they are now frustrated, even though they know very well, just like the rest of us, that this will not make the elevator come any sooner? (Oh, I have done that too! We all have.) Our minds are funny like that. They make us do the same things over and over again, even though we know that it makes no sense, and then with increased intensity, and get very frustrated when we get the same result. Let's stop doing that! Let's stop letting ourselves be stuck in situations where we do more of the same and get upset, because surprise surprise—we get the same results.

Sometimes we are not even aware that we are doing more of the same, because we are too engulfed in it. So let's first of all define what doing more of the same means. Doing more of the same is not necessarily repeating the same action, but it *is* repeating things that belong to the same family of actions.

For example—

Reactions Group 1:
Arguing, crying, yelling, slamming the door, storming out, sending a nasty text/email.

Alternatives to Reactions Group 1:
Having a heart-to-heart conversation, using humor, using forgiveness, calm communication.

Reactions Group 2:
Not saving, spending, excessive giving, lack of financial planning, excessive use of credit cards, excessive borrowing.

Alternatives to Reactions Group 2:
Budgeting, writing down expenses, allocating credit card use for only certain expenses.

Reactions Group 3:
Emotional eating, overeating, careless eating, eating and regretting.

Alternatives to Reactions Group 3:
Joining a healthy eating plan, seeing a therapist, using techniques to reduce stress, loving yourself.

Reactions Group 4:
Not sticking to a workout schedule, finding fault in every workout or gym, finding reasons not to work out, shortening workouts because you are too busy.

Alternatives to Reactions Group 4:
Joining a workout group, finding a workout you love, writing a detailed workout plan and placing it on the fridge, setting fitness goals with a deadline.

Reactions Group 5:
Forgetting birthdays, forgetting meetings, being late on different occasions, having a messy house, overloading your inbox, having a messy desk, feeling overwhelmed, missing deadlines, not paying bills on times, not being able to find things.

Alternatives to Reactions Group 5:
Running a calendar with pop-up reminders, designating time for daily organization, setting alarms and reminders.

For every topic or challenge, more groups and more examples can be created. Are you doing more of the same, thinking that you are doing something different but in fact repeating the same patterns and expecting different results? If you are, it would explain your frustration. The only way out of that frustration is to try something completely different. Only then you can expect to see change.

#5

Be Willing to Pay the Price

"Good, better, best. Never let it rest. 'Til your good is better and your better is best."
—St. Jerome

Many people want to create change, talk about change, and crave change, but are not necessarily willing to pay the price for the change. We understand, on a rational level, that if we stay where we are and don't move on with change, we will stay behind. We will lose our competitive edge. We will not be able to keep up with a rapidly changing world and we will not have access to having more if we do not become more. And yet we dread it. The reason why we dread it is quite simple and yet very powerful: we are not necessarily willing to pay the price. Our brains conserve 20% of our energy on a daily basis. With change, there is more focus needed, more effort needed, more strategizing, more overcoming difficulty. In other words, changing our ways is something that our brains are not crazy about, to say the least. Our brains are pretty comfortable doing more of the same for the simple reason that it requires less energy and less effort. When you decide to change, you are working against your brain. The price tag here is high: more effort, more focus, hard work. Do you want what you want enough to be willing to pay it?

Commercials build heavily on our fantasy on eating the cake and leaving it whole, not paying the price and yet having drastic and immediate results. All we need to do is use this shampoo, use this diet or exercise-without-effort product, buy this program, or choose this money-making strategy, and before we know it—powerful results without having to work for them or give up on anything that our heart desires. If you stop and think for a minute, you will realize that on a rational level, you do not really believe any of this, and yet on an emotional level, you really want to and you may end up buying the product, program, or strategy.

Considering that everything you want comes with a price tag, the question is not if you can skip the price tag. The question is how much you really want it to be willing to pay the price for what you want. In every aspect of life, the bigger the goal is, the higher the price you will have to pay. Shortcuts are possible, but they will rarely lead to lasting change and are typically short lived. If you are not seeing the price tag on what you want, you are not taking a realistic look at it.

#6

Change Your Inner Narrative

"Only I can change my life. No one can do it for me."
—Carol Burnett

We all walk around with inner narratives in our minds about ourselves and our place in the world. Those narratives have a tremendous impact on how we conduct our lives and how confident we are to challenge ourselves in terms of our belief in our ability to succeed. Those narratives are typically created in our childhood, and they play a major part in the way we interpret reality and react to it, in the way we take on challenges, and in the way we handle obstacles. Positive narratives (we call those "Ascending Narratives") are narratives that build you. This is where you have a positive inner narrative about yourself, that you are a capable, powerful, and successful person, no matter what the circumstances are. It is a wonderful thing to be a person with an ascending inner narrative, because your belief in yourself will push you to go further than you thought was possible. If you are a parent, believe in your kids with all your heart, no matter what. Your power in shaping their inner narrative is critical to their success.

Descending inner narratives, on the other hand, are inner narratives that we are not good enough, that others are better than us—they are debilitating and limit our belief in ourselves. Descending inner narratives work against us and operate like weights around our ankles when we want to run.

Changing the inner narrative, while a process, is very possible and, in fact, critical to your success. What do you tell yourself about yourself? Descending inner narratives sound something like this:

- Things never work out for me.
- I am not good at relationships.
- I just don't have that kind of luck.
- Things always end up like that for me.

Life is not about what happens to you. Life is about how you react to it, and your inner narrative has tremendous impact on your reactions to events. While changing your inner narrative is a process, here is a simple trick to do it:

Step 1: Isolate the sentence or sentences that you keep repeating to yourself that you feel are weighing you down.

Step 2: Decide on alternative sentences, one or two, that encourage and highlight your power and capabilities, and keep repeating them to yourself, almost like a brainwash.

Step 3: Every time a doubtful narrative creeps into your mind, block it and repeat the new, powerful, and encouraging sentences multiple times. Believe in them, in a meaningful and powerful manner, and keep repeating them. Think of your narrative as a replaceable chip. Your narrative is not you. It is a chip that was placed in your head in your childhood, it has nothing to do with you and it is an external story about reality, typically created by your parents or other people in your life in the early stages of your life. If you don't like it, if it doesn't serve you well toward your goals, you can change it. It is completely doable.

#7

Minimize Distractions

*"I don't focus on what I'm up against. I focus on
my goals and I try to ignore the rest."*
–Venus Williams

The world around us, in our daily lives, is full of distractions. While we are working on creating a lasting change, the world does not stop, stress does not go away, our feelings and frustrations do not go away, our responsibilities still require our attention, life is too busy, and social media is out there grabbing our attention and focus just to top it all. Within all of that, change requires our utmost focus and effort. Distractions, in that sense, are at every corner. How do we then handle the distractions and stay focused on our goals and stay on the path toward success?

Here are five ways to stay determined, focused, and on the right path toward a lasting change in the face of distractions:

1. Plan your day the night before

Before you go to sleep, have the items that you need in order to succeed and stay on track for the next day ready. For example:

- Healthy lunch that is ready to be grabbed in the morning.
- List of items that you need to take with you the next day.
- Your gym outfit and sneakers handy by your bed.

- A list of tasks to accomplish.
- A short list of things to keep in mind or focus on.

2. Do the most difficult things first

Research has shown that our minds are at their best in the morning, and for that reason it is best if we tackle the toughest or most likely to be avoided tasks first. Once we have that out of the way, we won't have to worry about it (another waste of energy) for the rest of the day and can focus on other, less difficult or less intimidating tasks and get them out of the way as well.

3. Eliminate time wasters

In every situation, with awareness, you can identify what wastes your time. If it is a talkative co-worker, politely state that you would love to catch up later; if it is your phone, put it away; if it is social media, disconnect; and if you are wasting time because you are jumping from one thing to another and completely overwhelming yourself, stop now and make a quick and clear to-do list, and then follow it item by item and check off what you have completed. Time wasters can be other people, electronics, or your own behavior. Whatever it is, time is one of your most precious resources. You cannot waste it because before you know it, the day will be gone and you will have done very little to create lasting change. Looking to accomplish another step toward lasting change today? Put the phone away. Disconnect from unnecessary drama. Stop wasting time. It will make all the difference in the world.

#8

Baby Steps, Big Leaps

*"Concentrate all your thoughts upon the work at hand.
The sun's rays do not burn until brought to a focus."*
—ALEXANDER GRAHAM BELL

Baby steps and small changes are in fact much better than big drastic changes when it comes to lasting change. The reason is that small changes are very unintimidating and can be more easily sustained. You won't worry about them, you will always have the time and availability to follow up on them, and overall, their impact can be tremendous. Here are some small changes that you can make in your life today, that can go a long way in creating a lasting change. Circle the ones that you can commit to and place them in the form of a written note in a visible place such as your fridge or your desk. If you are looking to create small changes in your life that are not on this list, just write your own, and place them in a visible spot:

1. Create clear to-do lists.
2. Pledge to take the time to be present and listen.
3. Do one active thing a day—a walk, a jog, anything active to boost yourself mentally and physically.
4. Tell yourself every day what you are thankful for.
5. Listen or watch something inspiring and uplifting.
6. Get rid of clutter.

7. Pledge to stop dwelling on past mistakes. If they sneak up on you, remind yourself that you are in control of your thoughts and you can replace a thought that is harmful to you.

8. If you are wasting time on social media or media in general, stop. It is a bad habit.

9. Distance yourself from negative people

10. Write down your three goals for each day, as well as your three most important tasks, and check them off at the end of the day.

Consider this: you *can* create small changes, and you *can* stick to them. Every small change counts. The beauty of it is that when you are successful in implementing one small change, you will likely implement more small changes. Walls are built brick by brick, and before you know it, an entire wall is created. Every small change is a brick. Build it step by step, brick by brick, and you will get the highest, most beautiful view from the top.

#9

Expect Setbacks

"The game has its ups and downs, but you can never lose focus of your individual goals and you can't let yourself be beat because of lack of effort."
—MICHAEL JORDAN

W e often have this idea in our mind of a linear line of progress. In reality, progress has a lot of back and forth, a lot of struggle, a lot of setbacks. If success and progress were linear, it would have been a much easier ride. But they are not. And it is in these setbacks that our power of will is tested. Do we want what we want badly enough to push forward no matter what? One of the best strategies to deal with setbacks is to expect them to happen. This way, we are not taken by surprise as much when they happen, and we don't get as discouraged. Embrace the challenge. Embrace the setbacks and push through. They are a challenge to own. There are three common setbacks that you can expect to meet on your path toward change:

No Results, No Motivation:

It can be very challenging to keep motivation going over a long period of time, especially if we don't see results and don't get the satisfaction of seeing progress. If you do not see the results that you expect, and feel that this is demotivating you, start tracking your progress in writing. If you write it down, you will see one of the following two things—your expectation is not realistic and you should adjust it (you started a diet three days ago and you are discouraged because you did not lose weight), or you did make progress but you have dismissed it (you did read 100 pages of the book, you did pass two courses, you did manage to do great things, but you chose to focus on what you did NOT do).

Self-sabotage:

Self-sabotage is patterns of behavior where you just ruin it for yourself. The origins of self-sabotage vary, and digging deep into where these behaviors came from will not necessarily solve them. What will help you tremendously with self-sabotaging behaviors is to recognize the patterns. See if you recognize yourself in any of these examples:

Procrastination:
- Knowing that you should be working on something but putting it off over and over again.
- Starting projects and not finishing them.
- Feeling unable to proceed even though you are doing well and making progress.

Self-Negativity:
- Criticizing yourself to the point that you feel discouraged.
- Fearing that if you fail, people will not like or appreciate you anymore.
- Doubting yourself and your capabilities.

Anger:
- Using aggressiveness rather than assertive communication
- Destroying relationships with anger, jealousy, and/or resentment.

Wasting time:
- Spending time focusing on small and unimportant things.
- Spending time worrying over things that really do not matter.
- Not getting things done, procrastination.

The first step in breaking the cycle of self-sabotage is recognizing your own self-sabotaging patterns. These are behaviors that typically come from bad habits, and bad habits can be replaced by good habits, once the awareness of the pattern is there. That honesty with yourself about your own patterns of behavior, and the realization of where they lead you, is critical to your success.

#10

Master Your Fears

"You gain strength, courage and confidence by every experience in which you really stop to look at fear in the face. You are able to say to yourself: 'I lived through this horror. I can take the next thing that comes along.'"
—ELEANOR ROOSEVELT

Your fears are the biggest sticks in your wheels, and you can rightfully consider them your biggest obstacle. Fear truly stands in our way of experiencing life in its fullest form and living to our fullest potential. Mastering your fears will open new doors and new opportunities for you, and it is important that you realize that your fears' control over your actions is no more than a state of mind. When we let fear dictate our choices, we have a false and completely misguided notion of being more protected, but the truth of the matter is that one of the most important things to accept about life is that life is dangerous and unexpected; we cannot always make sense of it and we certainly cannot control it. Any attempt to control life's circumstances hoping to stay in a safe bubble only limits our opportunities to grow and does not necessarily provide us more protection and certainty.

Our brain loves certainty and hates the unknown. As children, we like to hear someone say in a confident voice: 'Everything will be ok.' But nobody knows if everything will be ok. It is an illusion that we want to believe. If certainty is an illusion and safety cannot be guaranteed (you can sit in a bubble at home all day, and even then it is not guaranteed—and who wants that kind of life anyway?). Let's face our fears and move beyond them.

Fear is identified in a more primitive part of the brain in the limbic system called the amygdalae. It triggers emotional and impulsive behaviors and causes us to be in very little control of our actions and choices. When we are able to deal with fear effectively, the rational part of the brain takes over (the prefrontal cortex), and this is where we make better decisions and strategize our actions, rather than responding to events and people in an impulsive manner.

Here are three steps to master and curb your fears, so that you can live the life you want to the fullest, and perform at your best:

Step 1: Verbalize it.

Verbalizing the fear makes it specific and gives it form. It is the vagueness of fears that makes them seem bigger than they are and gives them their debilitating impact. Once we name them, we clarify what we are dealing with, and it makes it easier to address.

Here is what fears may look like when we verbalize them:

- The work won't get done.
- I am afraid that I will fail.
- I will run out of money.
- I will get fired.
- My kid will not do well at school.
- I will become a joke.
- I will be embarrassed in front of everybody.
- My family will not accept me.
- My spouse will not love me anymore.

Step 2: Share it with your loved ones.

Fear becomes much bigger when you hold it within you and do not share it with others. On many occasions, when you verbalize it and then share it with people who are close to you and whom you trust, it really doesn't seem that big anymore. Talk about it. Never hold it within you, no matter what it is.

Step 3: Check how it impacts you.

It is ok to be afraid. The question is only how it impacts you. The intensity of fear—anything from a concern, to troubling fears, to anxiety, to phobias—makes a big difference in how it impacts you, but what makes an even greater difference is what you do about it and how you manage it. Remember, fear goes hand in hand with change, and change goes hand in hand with growth. In that expect, it is to be expected. We cannot eliminate it, but we can make it concrete and by doing so eliminate its debilitating impact, and we can also control its intensity either by ourselves (meditating, listening to or reading something inspiring and uplifting, talking about it with someone who is close to us) or with professional help (therapist, coach, psychiatrist, mentor).

You are the one in control of your thoughts. You are the one in control of your actions. If you feel that fear is debilitating you, stopping you, or slowing you down, seek support, get professional help, get in control. You manage fear, not the other way around. These are the rules of the game if you are looking to hit the change button, and fear will have to play by your rules.

#11

Let Go of the Past

"I like the dreams of the future better than the history of the past."
—THOMAS JEFFERSON

Working toward change is working toward a different future. And if a better future is what you have in mind, you have to leave the past in the past. Being stuck in the past entails no movement forward. Often, past struggles sit heavy on our shoulders and hold us back from both living in the moment and moving forward at the speed that we want and deserve. According to research, holding on to our past is something that we tend to do because it contributes to our sense of identity. We are reluctant to let go of the past and cling to it, because as negative as it may make us feel and as painful it is, it is part of our who we are. By doing that, we allow negativity, anger, and fear to take over our mind and shape our energy and state of mind in the present. No more! Every day, every hour, and every moment are a new chance to let go, to dust the past away, and to make room for new energy, new experiences, and a new state of mind. Because we cannot change the past, it brings with it a sense of frustration. You will feel stronger and more hopeful if you drop that bag full of heavy rocks, your past, on the side of the road, and walk forward full speed, lighter and happier. Who wants to go run a marathon with a bag full of heavy rocks on their back? It is a deceiving sense of identity, because it works against you rather than for you. Here are three steps to move forward and create a new, winning, pain-free identity, and let go of the past:

1. Identify your habit of focusing on the past.

2. Train your mind to shift back to the present and be in the moment every time you drift back to past talk and past-oriented focus.

3. Once you are back in the present moment, envision the future that you are working toward in detail and linger on the pleasure that that future entails.

Leave the clouds of the past in the past. Turn your back on them and face the sun of the future. You cannot change the past. But you can just leave it where it belongs, in the past. And you can certainly change the future, so focus every bit of energy that you have on that.

#12

Set Your Goals High

"People with goals succeed because they know where they are going."
—Earl Nightingale

One of the most common mistakes when it comes to setting goals toward change is setting unrealistic goals. This is an important topic, because on the one hand, we do want to reach high and then higher, and setting challenging goals is important for us to get out of our comfort zone, but when we set goals that are just not realistic, we are setting ourselves up for disappointment that will ultimately discourage us. So how do we set the bar as high as possible and still set realistic goals that will not set us up for repeating failure?

Here is how you should look at it:

Above-realistic goals + realistic action plan = extraordinary results.

What does that mean? It means that you should set up goals that are beyond the ordinary and can take your life to a completely new level, but then put together an action plan that, even with a stretch, is realistic and can be followed up on within your life circumstances. I have set up many seemingly unrealistic goals in my life. I found that I was able to accomplish them with a series of action plans that were realistic within the reality of my life circumstances, and even with setbacks here and there, I was able to stick to my plan and make significant progress toward my goals. We can call it a high level of challenge within reason.

So what should be beyond what seems to be realistic? Your target result. This is where you challenge yourself to grow beyond what you think is even possible.

What should be challenging but realistic? Your action plan. Ask yourself: what matters to me the most? What do I really want? Be as concrete as you can and go beyond your current circumstances. When you think about it, use the term "take my life to the next level." That will bring you to a point of challenge within reason and take you to the next level in your life. From there, you can always climb up to the next one, using the same methodology.

#13

Use Doubt as Fuel:

"I love it when people doubt me. It makes me
work harder to prove them wrong."
—DEREK JETER

When you make up your mind to make a change in your life, there will always be those who blow negative winds around you. Whether those spreading negativity around you do it directly at you, through doubt and disbelief in you or in your ability to succeed, or indirectly, through spreading a vibe of negativity around themselves and engaging in negative and discouraging talk, you absolutely block that negativity from your life. Making a change in your life requires you to be positive and very optimistic about your future self, and any crack in that shield of positivity and optimism works against you. Often, negativity comes from those who are the closest to you, in a cover of supposable concern for your well-being. That kind of negativity is the most potentially harmful because it catches you in a soft spot and often completely off guard. The main impact of people who doubt you is in how they connect to your own inner narrative, and this is also where the solution is. If your inner narrative is of doubting yourself, their doubt will fuel your doubt and the result will be extremely harmful to your success. The more fragile your inner narrative is, the more you should block people who doubt you. However, if your inner narrative is strongly positive, you believe in yourself, you believe in your goal and in your plan no matter what, sometimes that doubt becomes fuel. You feel so sure about what you are doing that you gain motivation to prove your doubters wrong. This is the best position to be in. Whatever position you are in in terms of your inner narrative, work on becoming very aware of it. If your inner narrative is fragile, work on strengthening it. Strengthening yourself and your belief in your capabilities. Once that happens, the doubters either do not matter or become your fuel. Until that happens, do not expose yourself to doubters, because their impact might become a hazard to your inner narrative and therefore to your success.

#14

Embrace Constructive Criticism

"I like constructive criticism from smart people."
—PRINCE

The truth of the matter is that self-criticism, as well as criticism from others, is completely ok. This is where we reflect and have our checks and balances with ourselves. We do, however, need to differentiate between constructive and destructive self-criticism. One builds and the other destroys.

Here is the difference:

Constructive criticism:
- Focuses on situations, dynamics, reactions—not the person.
- Focuses on facts.
- Gives a person a door for learning, correcting, growing.
- Builds you up.

We *need* constructive criticism in order to get out of our comfort zone, as challenging as it may be to take sometimes, whether from ourselves or from others.

Destructive criticism, on the other hand, will:
- Attack the person, not the situation.
- Be biased.
- Be given impulsively.

- Be opinion based.
- Point out negatives and disregard the positives.
- Cause embarrassment.

When you have people in your life, personally or professionally, who can give you constructive criticism, embrace it and appreciate it. Learn from it and be open to it. Do not be defensive. Everybody can learn and grow from constructive criticism. We do not always see ourselves the right way; we make mistakes, and if we have someone that cares enough to help us see them in a caring and constructive way, it has tremendous growth potential for us. Appreciate it, do not be too proud to accept it, use your own judgement once you hear it. You can hear it and accept none of it, some of it, or all of it, but hear it out with an open mind and without pride or self-justification. It may have incredible value for you.

#15

Realize That Your Limits Are Nothing but a Mental Illusion

"Limits, like fear, is often an illusion."
—MICHAEL JORDAN

The idea that the limits that we impose on ourselves are nothing but a mental illusion and completely in our mind is hard to grasp. The challenges that we are facing are real—young children or elderly family members to care for, lack of money; lack of time, opportunity, or education; and this is just to name a few very reasonable, very understandable limitations. And yet some defy all rules, and manage to create a change against all odds, in spite and in the face of their circumstances. How come?

This struggle, between what you think you can do considering your circumstances and what you can actually do, is there, and it's real, and no one can defy it by you. If you share your limitations with others, they are likely to justify your difficulty to change your circumstances—within your circumstances. Other people justifying the limitations you believe you have does not promote change. Those limits that you believe that you have are all part of an inner narrative that you have, a perception of yourself and a perception of the world, that is completely subjective. It comes from your upbringing, from your self image, from your perception of what life is and how things work, which are completely in your mind and completely interchangeable. In that respect, it is not the circumstances, not the actual daily challenges that matter, but those subjective limits in your mind that will determine what you can and cannot do. Like everything else, to change the perception of your limits in your mind, you need to first recognize what they are. What is the story that you tell yourself about your limits, and where did it come from? Once you are able to answer those questions, you will be able to ask yourself if that story about your limits can be challenged and then changed. You see, there is no glass ceiling. It is imaginary. You, with your own mind, are the one who placed it there. And you, with your own awareness and power of will, are the one to lift it higher.

#16

Stop Finding Excuses

"He that is good for making excuses is seldom good for anything else."
—Benjamin Franklin

The main problem with making excuses for not challenging ourselves the way we were hoping for or planning for is that they undermine our accountability, which is the basis for all change. We cannot change if we do not hold ourselves accountable to our own choices, and if we make excuses, we mask our accountability, which then becomes our #1 barrier to change.

I find that the main reason for making excuses is a form of pride. When we mess up, and we know that we have messed up, we try to rationalize our behavior so that we do not have to tell each other the unpleasant truth—we have messed up. We love feeling good about ourselves. We love getting compliments and we love telling ourselves that we are overall wonderful, that if something doesn't work out, it is because we are some kind of heroic victims of a very difficult situation and we definitely prefer not to tell ourselves the truth: we were getting too comfortable, we did not work hard enough, or we just did not do a good enough job. There will always be challenges. Challenges are not the issue. Accountability to doing our very best in every given situation is the issue. Is it hard? Definitely. Is it humbling to acknowledge it when we mess up? Absolutely. But anything short of that will take us in endless circles of needing to make excuses for the simple reason that very little progress will be achieved.

Excuses are about saving face. Letting go of the bad habit of making excuses is about letting go of pride. It is through a humble attitude that we admit our mistakes, stop kidding ourselves by making excuses, and from there, grow. Tell yourself this: I let go of pride. I am brave to acknowledge whatever comes my way. I am accountable. I am powerful. Excuses are for the weak. Repeat as needed.

#17

Be Clear and Thorough in Whatever You Do

"The way that I work is very specific, very thorough, and the process has to be totally clear."
—Lynn Collins

Being clear and being through are two different ends of the same stick. Both are equally important. When you do something, and you want to do it very well, very thoroughly, and produce the best quality of work no matter what it is—sales, fitness, nutrition, marketing, renovating a house, managing a project—no matter what is in front of you, you need to be very clear on what the task is, what the details are, and leave no stone unturned without fully understanding it. What it means, in simple terms, is no cutting corners. Cutting corners is easy. It's tempting. We have already discussed the fact that the brain conserves 20% of our energy and that every new piece of information, every additional effort, anything new to focus on, is additional effort, something that your brain is not really crazy about. But every time you cut corners, you are taking a risk. Think of cutting corners like crossing the street without clearly and thoroughly checking that there are no cars coming your way. Would you do it? Would you cut corners on that? I hope not. Every time you cut corners, you are taking a similar risk.

Ask yourself:

- Am I clear about what I am doing?

- Did I produce the best possible result that I could have produced?
- Can I do better?

Now, you do have to prioritize. Not everything in your life can be done to perfection; that is not a realistic expectation. But when you have an important task at hand, something that is meaningful in your life, something that is critical to your success and can take your life to the next level—health, career, whatever it may be—do not allow yourself not to be clear on the process, and do not allow yourself not to be thorough. The effort you put in will pay back big time. Do not cut corners on the important things in your life.

#18

Don't Lose Your Calm

"Mistakes and pressure are inevitable; the secret
to getting past them is to stay calm."
—Travis Bradberry

Keeping your cool is essential to your success. Not because emotions are not valid or important. But because emotions cause you to act impulsively in situations where if you stopped and thought of what you were doing, you would have made different choices. How many times do we hurt the people that we need the most in our lives in order to succeed, just because we have acted impulsively or out of anger or emotion? How many times did you write emails that you shouldn't have, write texts that you shouldn't have, say things that you shouldn't have, or take hasty and much-regretted decisions? Making decisions, any kind of decisions, while being consumed by anger or emotion, is equivalent to drunk driving. There is no sober and responsible driver in the driver's seat. Is that how you want to make decisions? Using the same example of drunk driving, the right thing to do is to pull over. Do the same when you feel that you are consumed by strong emotions. Pull over. Don't drive. Don't text. Don't email. Don't say the first thing that comes to your mind. You will regret them later. When you are consumed by emotion, you are not in control. You are saying and doing things without any thought. You may come across as insensitive, hurtful, demeaning. You will definitely not accomplish any goals. The only goal that you will accomplish by acting out of emotion is an outlet to your feelings. Well, that's very nice for a minute, but it will not make you feel any better later and will be very difficult to fix. If you are dealing with a lot of pressure, if you are angry at yourself and others, if you are mortified by a setback or just upset at what is going on—breathe. Do not act when you are in that state of mind. Give yourself the time to calm down. When you feel that you are more calm and less emotional, you can weigh your options and take action. Not before you get to that state of mind. With a calm and composed mind, you are at your best and can handle whatever comes your way as the best form of yourself.

#19

Hold Yourself Accountable

"Accountability breeds response-ability."
—STEPHEN COVEY

Holding yourself accountable is the #1 key to hitting the Change button in your life. To understand how much accountability matters to your success, let's look at what accountability actually means. To be accountable means to be responsible for something that is within your control. Now let's look at the opposite of accountability—not taking responsibility for things that are actually within your control, and making excuses. Lack of accountability is when you blame others for your lack of success: your parents, your ex, your spouse, the government, or the weather. Anyone will be held responsible but not you. It is convenient to blame others, because it excuses us from taking responsibility and owning up to our actions. The simplest tool for holding yourself accountable is to write down what you need to do and by when, and then hold yourself accountable against what you have written down. If you wrote a list of things to get done, did you do them? If you wrote a list of tasks, did you follow up? If you challenged yourself and then wrote down your challenge, were you able to do what you challenged yourself to do? Writing things down is a simple and yet very powerful tool, because whatever is in our mind we can twist and turn and deny, but what we wrote down is there, looking at us from the paper and asking us: did you do that? The #1 problem of today's world is that on the one hand, life became more challenging, more demanding, and more difficult to handle, and on the other hand, people are far less accountable for their own shortcomings. Holding yourself accountable is taking ownership of your life, your mistakes, your setbacks, and your growth.

#20

Learn to Identify Patterns
and Change Them

*"If you don't like something, change it. If you
can't change it, change your attitude"*
—MAYA ANGELOU

Our behavior tends to repeat itself in different forms. Unfortunately, the vast majority of the time, we are unaware of our own repeating behavior patterns. What we are aware of is our frustration from feeling stuck. One of the best benefits of psychotherapy is that, through therapy, people discover their own behavior patterns. Once they do, they can take active steps toward changing those behavior patterns that were, up to that point, completely subconscious. Even without therapy, you may be able to identify some of your repeating behavior patterns.

Here are some common recurring, negative behaviors people deal with in their lives on a day-to-day basis. If any of the incidents below have happened to you at least five times, then it's likely to be a pattern attributable to you:

- Being late for appointments
- Not meeting deadlines
- Being absent-minded
- Getting together with the "wrong" partner, resulting in destructive relationships

- Sleeping late/not being able to wake up early
- Emotional eating
- Not exercising even though you planned to
- Getting into arguments or losing your temper
- Giving up halfway through whatever you're doing
- Selling yourself short within relationships
- Over-giving due to low self-esteem
- Staying back late at work; getting burnt out

Here is a short but powerful strategy to change your behavior patterns:

Step 1: List (in writing) the past five times you have been in a similar situation.

Step 2: Identify the commonalities of those situations.

Step 3: Drill down into the cause of the pattern.

Step 4: Identify three action steps to address the cause.

Remember, recognizing a behavior pattern in your life is 80% of the work done. Most people go about life not realizing their behavior patterns at all. It takes guts and awareness to identify your own repeating behavior patterns. You have just taken a super important step!

#21

Celebrate Small Wins

"Celebrate what you want to see more of."
–Tom Peters

Small wins are the stepping stones toward our biggest goals. Conquering those small wins takes such courage and determination because they are just the stepping stones, and we may lose sight of the bigger picture. Here is an interesting way to look at celebrating small wins that will completely transform how important you consider them: winning, like cigarettes, caffeine, and late-night munching, is habit forming. Once we begin to recognize small wins by celebrating them, the brain wants more of them. In that sense, to the brain, they become an addictive habit. The brain will then work consistently toward winning as much as it can be wired to want more coffee, more cigarettes, or more snacks. The question then becomes not if the brain can be programmed, but if you can outsmart your brain and program it toward change, personal development, and success. The answer is absolutely yes, and the better you get at celebrating small wins, the more likely you are to accomplish that. When you celebrate small wins you are working toward forming a habit of success. Too often, we tend to focus on what not accomplished yet, or what still needs to be done. Not to take away from the importance of those, to actually train ourselves to succeed, every small win counts, and every small win should be celebrated. It is an opportunity not only to be kind to yourself and encourage yourself, but also to train your brain to increase the frequency of successes and wins. What you focus on is what you will see more of. It's just how life works. Celebrate small wins and the big wins will follow. Every small win counts. How to celebrate small wins is completely up to you. You can communicate them, acknowledge them, or reward and treat yourself. Everybody is different in how they like to celebrate small wins, and there is no cookie cutter system here. Ask yourself: How am I going to celebrate small wins? How will I treat myself? What will work best for me? Once you are able to answer those questions for yourself, put yourself on your own system of recognizing small wins, just so that you do not end up overlooking and neglecting to celebrate them. Every win counts on your journey of forming habits of success.

#22

Challenge the Status Quo

"The manager accepts the status quo; the leader challenges it."
—Warren Bennis

Accepting the status quo is the exact opposite of hitting the Change button. Whatever that status quo may be—your financial circumstances, the way you live, your fitness and health, your relationship, your career, or just the way life is for you in general. The status quo of your life is a mere reflection of your state of mind and attitude. When your attitude becomes that of challenging your life circumstances, questioning why things turn out for you the way they do, why you end up getting the same results over and over again, you are already taking the first step toward change in your life. Often, the main problem is just accepting the status quo as is, not questioning it and instead just making peace with it. Who created that status quo? Where did it come from? Who said that it is a given? I'll tell you who said it. You. And you, by the same token, are also the one to challenge it and create a new reality for yourself. Here are three steps for questioning the status quo of your life:

Step 1: Ask yourself: Am I getting the same results over and over again?

Step 2: Ask yourself: Am I doing more of the same? What am I doing that lands me in the same position time after time?

Step 3: Ask yourself: What can I do that would be different?

Write down your answers. Hold yourself accountable to what you are jotting down on that paper in response to those questions. If what you wrote shocks or scares you, let it sit. Come back to it later, but don't sweep it under the rug. This is where your change potential lies. This is where you pick up the process of challenging the status quo. That status quo is something that you have created for yourself. It is in your hands to change it.

#23

Externalize Your Problems

"Problems are not stop signs. They are guidelines."
—Robert S. Schuller

Externalizing problems is a powerful tool for dealing with them. What often happens to us is that we identify the problems that we are dealing with, with ourselves or with the other person. This can get very hard to resolve. It causes us to blame others, blame ourselves, feel guilt, or just feel completely overwhelmed. When you separate the problem from the person, it becomes less personal and much easier to deal with. It is a simple and yet incredibly powerful way of tackling problems without getting emotional, without blaming and accusing, and without getting overwhelmed, and you will find it very helpful both in your personal and in your professional life. Externalizing the problem means that we call the problem by a certain name and treat it as a separate entity. We don't look at people as difficult or problematic, we look at the interaction as problematic. You can't change people, but you can change dynamics. Here are some examples of how you can shift from internalized problems to externalized problems:

My sister doesn't get me.	We have a communication problem.
My kids don't take me seriously.	We have a discipline problem.
I am a mess.	I have an organization problem.

Nobody appreciates what I do.	I have a problem in highlighting my contribution.
I am completely alone.	I need to solve my social problem.
Nobody cares about me.	I need to improve my support system.

See the difference? Once you externalize the problem and turn it into a noun, it is separate from you and becomes a challenge that needs to be resolved. It gets you out of the victim mode, and away from blaming and guilt. You will be hitting the Change button every time you use it, and you will see tremendous improvement in the way you approach anything in your life that you are looking to solve or improve.

#24

Find Your Tribe

"The best thing to hold onto in life is each other."
—AUDREY HEPBURN

We all crave being part of a group. We have been tribal by nature since our caveman days, when being part of a tribe was detrimental to our survival. In modern life, we are becoming increasingly disconnected from other people. Without our tribe, we often end up feeling distanced, depressed, spiritually disconnected, and even sick.

Social connection improves physical health and psychological well-being. A large number of studies show that people who have strong social connections also have higher self-esteem, are more empathic to others, and are more trusting and cooperative, and, as a consequence, others are more open to trusting and cooperating with them. Social connectedness generates a positive feedback loop of social, emotional, and physical well-being. Unfortunately, the opposite is also true for those who lack social connectedness. Low social connection has been generally associated with declines in physical and psychological health as well as a higher propensity to antisocial behavior that leads to further isolation.

To be successful, you need your tribe, whether big or small. You need the support of others around you and you need to feel that you are a part of something that is larger than yourself. That can be your family, your circle of friends, your church or synagogue or any other social platform where you can be connected with others. Do not allow yourself to be isolated. You need others in your life. When you connect with the people that matter to you the most in your life, when you strengthen those connections and expand your tribe, your support and connection group, you become stronger. You become more powerful than one person is. You have the power and energy of a group.

#25

Turn Off the Autopilot

*"Let us not look back in anger, nor forward
in fear, but around in awareness."*
—JAMES THURBER

Our brain loves autopilot. The reason for that is that when we are on autopilot, which is the opposite of being mindful, the brain spends less energy. Our limbic system, which is the most primitive part of our brain, is responsible for all of our automatic decision making. This includes things like responding to traffic signs, checking our emails occasionally, or loading the dishwasher. These are actions that we do without much mental effort. They are trivial and do not require executive skills such as planning, focusing, and strategizing. Our prefrontal cortex, which is the more modern and sophisticated part of our brain, is the part responsible for focusing, creative thinking, and willpower. This requires energy and effort, and none of these are on autopilot. In our everyday life, about 45% of our decisions come from our primitive brain. We naturally want to conserve our mental energy, so we subconsciously default to that type of decision-making mechanism whenever we can. This is great for brushing teeth and loading the dishwasher, but the problems start when we use it for more complicated decisions without even realizing it. This causes us to make poor decisions which we then later regret. We would not have made these decisions had we been more mindful, focused, and aware. There are two main strategies for keeping our more primitive part of the brain at bay, becoming more mindful, and making great decisions rather than being on autopilot:

Meditation

Meditation trains the modern part of our brain, the prefrontal cortex, to be present. Practicing meditation for as little as 10 minutes a day will help develop your natural ability to focus and let go of worries about the future or the past. Simply by training the brain to be present in the decision-making process, you will naturally begin to think about the decision with your modern brain.

Self-Monitoring

Self-monitoring means keeping track of as much information about yourself, such as tasks and goals, as possible. The best way to do this is to write everything down and then check yourself against your own lists. Like with the mirror, you will look at the information on yourself and compare it to what you really want. This will turn on your modern brain and train it to take over in your decision-making process.

#26

Your Future Is In Your Hands

"Change your future today. Don't gamble on
the future, act now, without delay."
—SIMONE DE BEAUVOIR

Here is the best part of it all. Your future is in your hands. You can shape your future with your thoughts and attitude, you can shape it with the choices that you make, you can shape it with the decisions that you take. Nobody else holds the key to your future but you. Now, are there certain circumstances that may come your way that are beyond your control? Of course. You cannot control the ebb and flow of life. You cannot control the global economy, or the weather, or whatever life may throw at you. But here is the great news: you can control the path you choose for yourself. You can control your focus. You can control your goals and your plans and how much of them you will accomplish. Isn't that wonderful? It is remarkable how much power we have in our hands. Far more than we sometimes realize. And so what do we do with that power that we have, to shape our lives, to determine our future? We respect it. We value the choices that we have. We value and respect our strength and our opportunities. If you are not where you want to be in life, change it. Change direction. Change your plan. Change your attitude. Change the way you manage your life. If you feel powerless, it is because you made the choice to feel powerless. It is because it is convenient to you to feel that way. It is not the absolute truth. There are no circumstances that will make you powerless other than your own choices. It is all within your choices and your control. If you do not want to find yourself in five, ten, fifteen years exactly where you are now, going in circles and reaching the same, or similar results, it is in your hands to choose a different attitude, make different choices, manage your life differently. It is in your hands what you choose to do tomorrow, and every other day of your life, this month, this year, and beyond. It is in your hands how you choose to manage your life.

#27

Every Day Counts

*"Success is not final, failure is not fatal; it is the
courage to continue that counts."*
–WINSTON CHURCHILL

When you are working to create the life that you want, to turn your life around, to change your life for the better, every day counts. We don't have unlimited time on this planet, and in fact, we don't know at all how much time we have. Time is a sneaky thing; if you do not watch it, it slips right between your fingers. So time should be managed. Don't let hours be wasted, days be wasted, years be wasted, when you can use that time to do things that are important to you, that can change your circumstances and help you get to where you want to be. Here is a simple trick that you can use to make every day count toward your progress: write down on paper three things that must happen on that day to help you move toward your goals. These are not daily chores. These are three things beyond your day-to-day to-do list. A phone call that you have been putting off. Paperwork that you need to send that is important for your success. A book that you need to read. A course that you need to sign up for. Three forward-pushing things, as small as they may be, per day. By the end of the day, check them off. By now, you not only made progress on that day, you also know exactly what it was. You can feel great about it, and plan your progress for tomorrow. If life got in your face and you did not get those three things done, get one done and push the other two to tomorrow. Push something forward every day. Every day counts.

#28

You CAN Figure It Out

"If somebody offers you an amazing opportunity but you are not
sure you can do it, say yes. Then learn how to do it later."
–RICHARD BRANSON

The ability to be resourceful is the ability to tap into your inner resources—your knowledge, your skills, your creativeness—to come up with solutions to the problems that you face. Because problems and challenges are inevitable, the question then becomes not how to live a life that is free of problems, but how to be the most resourceful person that you can possibly be in order to deal with them. This is what will make all the difference in the world for you. Here are the four basic strategies for being the most resourceful that you can be. Practice them, and your increased resourcefulness is guaranteed to improve your success in every aspect of your life:

1. Operate both from within the system, and from outside of it.

Realize that in some situations the solution comes from working your way within the system, while in other situations you will have to bend the rules. This does not mean that I am advocating for anarchy. This means that I am advocating for creativity, entrepreneurship, and independent thought.

2. Be openminded

The best advice can come from the most unpredictable people. The best solutions may be completely out of the box. It is ok to break boundaries and define to yourself what is and isn't possible. Being openminded will allow you to find remarkable value not only in unpredictable people, but also in different events and circumstances. Expand your thinking to realize that there is value in every experience, in every person, in every circumstance.

3. Remember how competent you are

You must believe in your capability to handle any problem that is thrown on your plate. Your belief in your capability to be resourceful and solve problems will provide you with unusual capabilities to be resourceful in different situations. The truth of the matter is that you have all of the information that you need in order to solve any problem, and if you do not have it, you have the ability to figure out where to get it. You just need to believe in yourself that you can, and you will.

4. Always be proactive

If you are facing a problem, the last thing you should care about is why it happened and whose fault it is. This backward, past-oriented type of thinking is a shift away from resourceful thinking. Resourceful thinking does not care whose fault it is. It is solution-oriented and cares about how to solve the problem. In that respect, it is forward facing. Train yourself to always be proactive. Keep your thoughts solution-focused and facing the future.

#29

You CAN Control Your Thoughts

"The greatest weapon against stress is our ability
to choose one thought over the other."
—William James

One of the most common human mistakes about thinking is that thoughts are something that we cannot control. Your thoughts are not real, they are only real in the way they impact how you feel, and as a result, your actions. Think of your mind as an empty box, ready to receive any thought that you are welcoming into it. Because thoughts are not real, you do not and should not accept them as a given. You can welcome a thought, reject a thought, or change the course of a thought. Just the realization that you have the power to accept and reject certain thoughts is in itself very empowering. Do not think of it in terms of trying to be more positive, because this basically means that you are allowing or even welcoming negative thoughts into your mind and then fighting them. Decide to recognize a negative thought when it comes your way as something external to you that is negative and harmful to you, and then decide that you are not letting it in. That you have the power to think something else. You can decide what food goes in your body. You can decide what thoughts you are letting into your brain and what you are deciding to brush out. By letting good thoughts into the box of your brain and brushing away the negative ones, you are influencing your feelings, and as a result, the actions and decisions that you are going to take.

Viktor Frankl has said:

"Between stimulus and response there is a space. In
that space is our power to choose our response. In our
response lies our growth and our freedom."

**Knowing that you are not your thoughts puts that space between
the stimulus and your response.** The next time you run into a disturbing
thought or emotion, remember that it does not define or control you. You
can actively choose whether to participate in it or not.

#30

Expect Challenges and Eat
Them for Breakfast

"Expect problems and eat them for breakfast."
—ALFRED A. MONTAPERT

Many times, the main problem with a challenge is that it takes us by surprise. We have a false expectation for things to go smoothly, and then we get extremely disappointed when they do not. Do not kid yourself thinking that you will be so out of the ordinary that your ride will be smooth. Do not kid yourself thinking that everyone else has a smooth ride, but you are the only one or one of the only few having problems, challenges, and difficulties. That perception is in your mind and it is not true. Everyone has problems, everyone has challenges, and if someone has smooth sailing one minute for one thing, they will face a challenge, a problem, or an obstacle in the next. There are no exceptions to that. It is just how life works. So when life hits you with a challenge, no matter what it is, don't be mad at being challenged any more than you are mad at the snow falling or the wind blowing. Challenges and problems that need to be solved are a part of how life works, and though you never know what challenges will come your way, hope for the best, prepare for the worst, and do not be angry, upset, or disappointed when they come, because they come one way or another for everybody. The question is how skilled you are at "eating them for breakfast," how skilled you are in solving problems and how determined you are not to give up.

Here are three steps to crush your next obstacle (and eat it for breakfast):

1. Accept and Acknowledge It:

Let go of your fears, stress, and frustration about what is happening and the people who are involved in it. Even if you think that someone is to be blamed for the situation, it really does not matter. Feeling angry toward that person will not help you resolve the situation.

2. Observe, Analyze, Decide:

Observe and analyze the situation without letting your emotions take over. Look at the facts. Decide what the best approach is to handle it and react.

3. Be Thankful for the Challenge:

In every situation, there is good. You may not see it now, or you may be able to see it but choose not to see it, but there is good in everything. Find it, be thankful for what you have, with and around your challenge, and dwell on that gratitude. Focusing on what is good will bring more good.

#31

Ask Yourself: What Does Success Mean for Me?

"The best and most beautiful things in the world cannot be seen or even touched—they must be felt with the heart."
—Helen Keller

The differentiation between wants and needs is a tricky one. We are exposed to a consumer culture that makes it hard for us to even separate these things. We have been taught from a young age that accumulation of things is better. The more stuff we have, the better we are. The psychology of these things cannot be understated; we need to dig deep into ourselves to examine our motivations. A lot of research has been done on what people need the most in order to be happy. Most of the research on this points to the same results—people need a sense of purpose, a sense a community, and a sense of belonging. And yet there is a need for each of us to define our own definition of what success means for us, what matters to us the most. Defining that for ourselves gives us clarity as far as why we do what we do and why we invest so much of our time, resources, and efforts into it. Never judge others for their definition of success. It is hard to understand other people's rationales, life circumstances, and thinking processes. But take the time to define your success to yourself. To define your 'Must,' you need to better understand what success means for you. If you're focusing on what everyone else's idea of success is, you'll never achieve it. Success, like beauty, starts from the inside out.

You have to dig inside yourself to define your own version of success. Not what your friends think, nor your family, not even the entrepreneurs and business leaders you look up to.

You can take tips from the important people in your life. Go ahead and borrow best practices. But you have to discover what your own definition of success is to achieve it. Why try to live someone else's dream while standing in the way of your own? The definition of success is steady progress toward a clearly defined goal. What is the goal that you are working toward? Are you making steady progress toward it? If so, you are successful, and as long as you continue to make steady progress, you will become increasingly more and more successful.

#32

See the Opportunity in Every Difficulty

"I can't change the direction of the wind, but I can adjust my sails to always reach my destination."
—JIMMY DEAN

O ften, people ask themselves, how do I recognize opportunity? How do I know it is coming? What if it passes right by me and I do not know when my next opportunity comes? You recognize opportunity by being attentive. Be attentive to people. Be attentive to your clients. Be attentive to your coworkers. Be attentive to trends. Be attentive to what is happening around you. Just quiet your fears, quiet what you think are other people's expectations, quiet any sense of anger, disappointment, or blame. And just listen. Be attentive, and in what you hear, you will find opportunity. Not by force, but by listening. From your calm and attentive mind, you will be able to connect the dots together. Opportunity will skip you if you are not listening to others, if you are not attentive to what is happening around you. Opportunity will skip you if you are focused on yourself. We are here living the life that we live not only for ourselves, not only for our own pleasure, but also because we can be of help to others. It is that connection between us and others, between us and the world around us, that attentiveness, that shift from the self to the self in connection to others, that will help us see the opportunity, connect to the opportunity, seize the opportunity. In every difficulty, there is an opportunity. In multiple situations around you, there are opportunities. Opportunity is all around you. Calm your inside noise. Shift away from ego, pride, blame, and expectations. Just listen, and be attentive. It will come your way.

#33

Never Let Rejection Discourage You

"A rejection is nothing more than a
necessary step in the pursuit of success."
–Bo Bennett

Rejection impacts us in several ways, and it is important to be aware of those impacts as you are working your way around dealing with them. On the most basic level, rejection causes us real pain: We can relive and re-experience social pain more vividly than we can physical pain. If you try to remember a time where you have experienced physical pain, you will probably have a recollection of it, but it will not cause you to actually relive that pain in the way you remember it. With a painful mental or emotional memory, just thinking of it will cause you pain again. So in dealing with rejection, we need to realize that we are dealing with something that is truly painful in our experience. Rejection shakes our self-esteem, because we often respond to rejection by finding fault in ourselves. We dig deep within ourselves to try to understand why we were rejected and what we did wrong. It Is hard to reason with rejection, because rejection and the feelings that accompany it are usually so strong that our reactions toward it do not respond to reason. But rejection happens, and the only way to avoid is not to try, not to aim high, not to take risks. Not exactly a recipe for success. Here are five ways to deal with rejection and move on without dropping your goals and steering away from the path that you have chosen for yourself:

1. Acknowledge how you feel about being rejected:

It's ok and normal to feel embarrassed, sad, disappointed, and discouraged. There is no point denying it or hiding it from yourself or others. If you were passed for a promotion, or rejected for a date, remind yourself that you are a capable and powerful person and that whatever you are feeling is ok—you will overcome it, like any other obstacle in your life.

2. Rejection is evidence for challenging yourself

Rejection is proof that you are challenging yourself, and that you are pushing your limits. It is proof that you took a shot at it. If you know someone who never got rejected, they are probably living deep in their comfort zone. Is that what you would choose for yourself?

3. Be kind to yourself

Don't give yourself a hard time over getting rejected. No negative self-talk, no self-criticism, no self-sabotage. Beating yourself up is the worst thing that you can do right now. Lift yourself up, talk to yourself as if you are your best friend on earth. Tell yourself that you are strong, capable, and powerful. That you can feel bad today, but tomorrow is a new day.

4. Rejection does not define you

Getting rejected is nothing but an incident. If you were not hired, it does not mean that you are incompetent. If you were dumped, it does not mean that nobody loves you. A single incident, or even several incidents, do not define you. They depend on circumstances and they depend on other people's opinions. Circumstances change, and there will always be other people who will think completely differently.

5. Rejection is a lesson

Ask yourself: What did I learn from this? How was this a learning opportunity for me? Sometimes you learn some things that you need to improve in. Sometimes you just learn to deal with rejection and move on. Whatever it is, embrace the lesson.

#34

Reach Out and Help Others

"We are all here on earth to help others; what on earth the others are here for, I don't know."
–W. H Auden

Research proves over and over again that giving and supporting others is a powerful means of personal growth and happiness. Giving stimulates the same pleasure areas of the brain as eating and having sex. In other words, helping others causes us a great amount of pleasure. Volunteering and giving to others often also leads to what is called "helper's high," which happens when doing something good releases feel-good hormones such as Oxytocin in your body, while lowering your stress hormones. So can money buy you happiness? Yes, if you use some of it on donating to others. The answer for our self-pleasure in giving has a lot to do with our need for purpose. Donating our time, money, or resources does not make us poor, but for someone else, it may mean the world. In helping, we have just made a difference in someone's life, and that gives us an incredible sense of purpose and value. Find ways to be valuable to someone. Find ways to make a difference that are unique to you. You have the power to help others, you have the power to make a difference. The greatest joy in life is not in chasing self-centered ambition relentlessly. The greatest joy in life is in making a difference.

#35

Take Control into Your Hands

"Be yourself. Take control of your life"
—EMMA BUNTON

One of the most powerless situations to be in is when you feel that you are being led, that you have lost control over your life. I remember my own father, a man used to being a top executive, running complex situations and being powerful and in control, sick with pancreatic cancer, and finding himself feeling weak not just by terminal cancer but by the situation that he found himself in: at the mercy of doctors and nurses, run by the situation, thrown between extremes. I will never forget sitting with him and reminding him who he was—a top executive, a skilled manager, a man of power. The minute he took the decision that from now on he was running the show, was the minute he regained his identity. No longer the cancer patient in hospital pajamas, but the man he was: powerful, capable, in control of the situation. He started managing the situation rather than being managed by it. He decided which doctors to work with, what choices he was making, what he wanted and how he wanted it. With that, until his last day, he kept his identity and held his head high. No matter what waves hit your boat, remain in control. Never let others determine things for you, as easy as it may seem. You can gain information from them, educate yourself as far as your choice, but hold the wheel and remain in control of your ship. This way, you steer it where you want to go. This way, you stay in control.

#36

Never Give Up

"If you fall behind, run faster. Never give up, never surrender, and rise up against the odds."
—JESSE JACKSON

If you know what you want and believe in your way and in what you do, there is nothing that should make you give up on what you are working toward, no matter how great the difficulty you are facing and how discouraged you may sometimes feel.

Here are seven reasons why you should never give up:

1. You are alive and you can:

As long as you are alive, there is no excuse why you cannot make your best effort, put your mind to it, and figure it out. In other words, if Christopher Reeve can do it, so can you.

2. You have everything you need:

Everything that you need in order to succeed is already within you. It is just a matter of working with the resources that you already have. Drop the excuses.

3. Success will feel great:

Imagine to yourself the minutes, days, and months of your success. What it will feel like, look like, taste like, sound like. Now go get it.

4. Things can change for the better, anytime:

Things may seem rough and challenging now, but everything can instantly change, and you never know when it will. You never know when you are going to hit a breakthrough.

5. You are strong, capable, and powerful:

You have the strength to do whatever you set your mind to do; no matter the setbacks, you have the power within you to keep at it.

6. You live and learn:

You learn so much by not giving up. You will definitely learn how to do things better, and you will also learn what you are good at and where you still need to grow. With every thing that you do not give up on, you become better.

7. It could be worse:

Be thankful for the situation that you are facing and think to yourself how it could be worse and how good it is that is it not at this worse point. There will always be people who have bigger problems than you.

#37

It Is Never Too Late

"It is never too late to be what you might have been."
—GEORGE ELIOT

It doesn't matter if you're 25, 35, 55, or 85—it's NEVER too late to change your priorities.

Because that's what creating the life you want is really about: changing your priorities. Making room for more meaning. Figuring out how to focus on what really matters to you the most. No matter how old you are when you realize you want do this, it often feels like it's too late. You may feel as if you have wasted the last two or five or ten or twenty or more years focusing on the wrong job, the wrong business, the wrong person, making choices that are not right for you. So here's the thing: It is not too late, and you definitely have not been wasting your time. Doing something different does not cancel your investment in your current path. It is all a part of your life's journey. The time you have invested in it is all a part of that journey. And no matter what, it is absolutely never too late to create the life you want. The reason for this is that you have the right to live a happy and fulfilling life every day of your life on this earth. And you always have tomorrow. And hopefully the next day, and the day after that. And each of those days is there for you to spend how you choose. The pure fact that they haven't yet happened, that they're *waiting for you*, means they hold so much more potential than what you've already done. Whatever obstacles or circumstances hold you back, it is your choice to allow them to hold you back. It doesn't matter what people say, or what you think they may say; the most important thing is to make the conscious choice of what your tomorrow and all the days that follow it will look like for you. You have the right to make that choice, no matter how you have spent the last few years and no matter how old you are. It is a fundamental human right: the right to choose your path, and the right to change it.

#38

Do Not Let Fear Dictate Your Limits

"There are no limitations to the mind except those we acknowledge."
—Napoleon Hill

The limits to what we can do, to who we can become, are imaginary limits created by our minds. They are dictated by our fears, and by our perception of ourselves, the way it was engraved in us since childhood. If we think that we are capable, powerful, and can accomplish great things, then it will be true. If we think that we are limited, powerless, and not capable of much, that will be just as true and will dictate our choices and as a result, our reality. Which would you rather define as your limits? If you are the one setting your own limits to what you can do, where do you want to set them?

Have you ever stopped to define to yourself what you think you can do? Imagine your life in five years from today. Where will you live? What will you do? Imagine your finances, your family, your home, your health, your lifestyle. Close your eyes when you envision this. Be detailed. Be daring. What are you seeing in your mind? That vision that you are seeing in your mind of your life five years from today shows you where you think your limits are. Those limits may stretch and extend themselves even further in the course of your life journey, but right now, at this point, your job is to believe that you can get to what you have envisioned, and work diligently, every day, on getting your life in that direction, and getting yourself there.

#39

The Power of Empowerment

*"When you think about growing and being
empowered yourself, it is what you've been able to
do for other people that leaves you the fullest."*
—OPRAH WINFREY

When you are working to empower yourself, you are basically telling yourself that you are capable and powerful in taking control of your life by making the right choices for you toward your goals. By understanding your strengths and weaknesses, you build on your strengths to overcome your weaknesses so that your weaknesses do not stand in the way of accomplishing what you are looking to accomplish. When you empower yourself that way, when you tell yourself that you are capable and powerful, and then connect your life to a purpose with passion, nothing can stand in your way. Empowerment is what blows the wind in your sails, as much as by empowering others, you blow the wind in their sails. It is the belief in our capabilities that encourages us to be more capable, more resilient, and more resourceful than we thought was possible. Because our self-image determines the way we act and the choices we make, enhancing that self-image, highlighting our strengths and encouraging a positive and powerful self-narrative, empowers us to set higher goals for ourselves and then go ahead and accomplish them. If you want to do the kindest thing for yourself, empower yourself by telling yourself over and over again how capable, resilient, resourceful, and powerful you are. If you want to do the kindest thing for others, look for opportunities to highlight great and remarkable things that they have done that basically make the same point. The road to success and growth from there just became shorter.

#40

Turn Negative Situations into Positive Ones

"Always turn a negative situation
into a positive situation."
—MICHAEL JORDAN

Accept complete responsibility for every situation in your life. Refuse to accuse and blame others. This is the first key in taking responsibility and ownership over any situation. Once you do that, you are already able to start turning the situation in any direction that you choose. It is the negative emotions that actually impact the situation more than the situation itself. Eliminate negative emotions in your control. Most of the negative emotions come from blaming others for a certain situation. You cannot change others, you cannot change the situation, but you can decide not to blame others and not to be negative. You cannot be responsible for other people, but you are always responsible for your reactions, your response. Take a deep breath. You are in control of your response at all times. Nobody can make you feel negative other than yourself, in the way that you think about the situation and process it in your mind. You have complete control of your thoughts, and as a result, of your feelings and subsequent actions. Blaming, accusing, and making excuses are all forms of lack of accountability and not taking responsibility for being positive about the situation no matter what the circumstances are. Check yourself. Does the situation feel very negative because you are blaming and accusing others? Can you look at the situation differently and accept responsibility by rejecting negativity? Will it feel different to you?

Here are two important tips for turning negative situations into positive ones:

1. Accept the situation and keep yourself solution oriented:

Many times, when dealing with a negative situation, people spend a tremendous amount of energy on sorrow. They ask themselves why it happened, think how unfair it is, and waste a lot of energy, while being completely overwhelmed. No matter how bad the situation is, to turn it around into something positive, you need to start by accepting it. We do not always know why things happen to us the way they do, and we may never find out, but we can control how we process them and what we do about them, and that is the source of our power within the situation. Once you have accepted the situation, all of your energy should be directed toward finding the best possible solution under the circumstances. This is how you shift from wasting energy to redirecting energy in a way that will help not only you but also the situation itself.

2. Train your mind to treat every negative situation as a life lesson:

When you train your mind to look at any misfortune that you have as a life lesson, you actually direct your energy in such a way that you clearly see what the life lesson is. In fact, when you train your mind to think that way, it will surface right up for you. You will not be able to miss it. If life is a series of lessons, take a student's approach and become the best version of yourself within the situation rather than complaining about it. This is exactly what you want to see your mind focused on. It will make you better, stronger, and definitely more successful.

#41

Share What You Learn

"If you have knowledge, let others
light their candles at it."
—Margaret Fuller

If you have learned certain things along your life journey, others can benefit from your knowledge. Never assume that your knowledge is trivial and cannot be beneficial to someone else. You never know what difference you can make in someone's life by sharing what you know with them. Here are three reasons to share your knowledge with others:

1. It will reinforce your memory:

Every time you share what you have learned with others, you will remember it better and it will becomes a part of you.

2. It will challenge your understanding:

Sharing your knowledge will force you to understand things better, to dig deeper, to consider some aspects of your knowledge that you may not have thought about. All of this makes sharing your knowledge no less helpful to you than it is to those that you are sharing your knowledge with.

3. It will encourage others to share with you:

There is something to be learned from everybody. When you share your knowledge, in that interaction, you will learn some things from others too. See it as a knowledge-exchange situation. You never know what knowledge will come your way from the other end, and it may be completely unexpected.

#42

Stay Focused

*"I find hope in the darkest of days and focus in
the brightest. I do not judge the universe."*
–The Dalai Lama

Focus is your most important and valuable resource. It determines your ability to stay on task toward your goals, whatever those goals are, against all of life's distractions. Life is full of distractions. Our everyday chores, our relationships, our responsibilities, our expectations of life and of ourselves, what we think are others' expectations of us. The truth of the matter is that it is easy for us not to focus, because focus requires effort and we are often too mentally tired from life's chores and difficulties to add the additional effort of having to focus and then refocus ourselves around our goals and around our plan and efforts to achieve them. How do we then keep ourselves focused while facing all of these distractions and, above all, our inner will to let go, to not focus, to be on autopilot? The best thing you can do to keep yourself focused is to write down your goals. Break them into smaller tasks and write those down too. You need to dedicate just five minutes a day to planning: planning your day, planning your week, writing down what needs to be down and breaking it down into smaller tasks. There is no way that you do not have five minutes a day to write down your goals and tasks for the day and follow up on those from the previous day. Start every day with a to-do list that aligns with your goals. One thing at least on your list has to push you forward toward your goals, beyond your day-to-day tasks. As you write your daily list in the morning or, preferably, the night before, ask yourself: What absolutely has to happen today to push me forward? Write it down and make sure to do it, no matter what.

#43

Train Yourself to Be Confident

"The most beautiful thing you can wear is confidence."
—BLAKE LIVELY

So how do you actually train your brain to be more confident? The best way to go about it is to use a psychological method called NLP (Neuro Linguistic Programming). NLP is a scientific method that boosts self-confidence by repetition of a confidence boosting phrase that people say to themselves about themselves and what they are capable of. This might seem crazy, but it works. Be positive, and repeat a simple empowering sentence to yourself. It will boost your confidence and have tremendous impact on how you carry yourself, because the way you talk to yourself influences your neurobiological response to it.

We use NLP, which is in essence powerful repetition of positive and empowering sentences, to help us think positively and overcome what is called The Negativity Bias. The negativity bias, also called The Negativity Effect, is our tendency to be more impacted by negative events or negative information compared to neutral or positive things. To boost your confidence and overcome The Negativity Bias, always remind yourself of at least three great things that you have done today, three ways in which you made progress. If you have a hard time finding those, and you find that you are focusing on the negative—what didn't work out or what you did not accomplish—go back to your daily goals and check yourself. If nothing worked out, it was just that kind of day. Make today's goals into tomorrow's goals.

Here are three simple steps for using NLP to train your brain to be more confident:

1. Identify the emotion that you want to stop feeling (fear, lack of confidence, feeling that others are better than you, etc.).

2. Reframe the feeling in an empowering sentence. For example:
   - I am capable and talented.
   - I can do this.

3. I am going to graduate/get this done/get through this—whichever is relevant to your situation specifically.

Use repetition to plant that sentence in your mind. Repetition is very important in replacing negativity in the brain. Think of it as a power wash of negativity out of your brain and planting flowers instead of dirt. Make the sentence that you are choosing to plant in your brain simple and powerful, and repeat it to yourself constantly. It will work.

#44

Shift Gears from Reactive to Proactive

"Recast your current problems into proactive goals."
—Suze Orman

Being proactive is all about taking charge, managing the situation rather than being managed by it. When you are reactive, you are simply responding to the situation. Once you shift from responding to the situation to being proactive, you can manage the situation rather than being managed by it. Here are five steps to shift gears from reactive to proactive and take control of your life:

1. Be solution focused:

Many times, people tend to focus on the problem rather than on its solution, without even realizing that they are doing it. This means that they waste their time dwelling on the problem, blaming others for the problem, being upset over the problem or overwhelmed by it, rather than putting their focus on finding a solution, no matter what caused the problem or whose fault it is. Taking a solution-focused approach will always allow you to find a solution quicker and in a more effective manner.

2. Stay consistent:

Being proactive is a mindset that requires consistency. It becomes a habit of setting goals and following up on them in a solution-oriented manner, rather than reacting to situations with emotions while focusing on the problem. Once you consistently get into the habit of taking a proactive approach, it will come naturally to you and will simply become your second nature in terms of how you handle life's challenges.

3. Separate your emotions from your actions:

Emotions make it hard to think clearly, and taking an emotional approach to challenging situations usually not only does not solve the problem, but also leads to impulsive reactions that at best waste your time that could have been used toward solving the problem and at worst make it worse. If you feel that you are very emotional, take a deep breath—or a few—and calm yourself down before you attempt to resolve anything. You will not be able to come up with proactive solutions before you calm yourself down.

4. Think through possible scenarios:

Focus on likely scenarios and create a plan. Plans can certainly change, but considering the most likely scenarios in advance will increase your chances of being prepared and remaining a step ahead of possible situations.

5. Take a forward-looking approach:

A forward-looking approach means that you leave the past in the past and do not dwell on why things happened or who is to blame for them. Whatever happened happened. The only thing that should be on your mind with a forward-looking approach is how to make it better from this point going forward. This is the healthiest approach to take to any situation.

#45

You Never Know When Opportunity Is Coming

"Success is where preparation and opportunity meet."
—BOBBY UNSER

We often feel discouraged because we feel that we have worked very hard, we feel that we deserve to succeed, but no breakthrough happened and we are still struggling. The truth of the matter is that we never know what's around the hill for us. We never know when opportunity and all the preparation, all the hard work that we have done, will meet. The greatest risk of that lack of knowledge is getting discouraged. It is hard for us to operate under uncertainty. Our brain loves certainty, and not knowing what to expect or when to expect it makes the brain anxious. How are we then to tackle it? How are we to keep ourselves motivated under conditions of uncertainty? The solution to that is not to look for certainty in a place where it doesn't exist. This will just leave you anxious and frustrated. The solution is to focus on a higher goal, a purpose for what you do, and just push through. If you do not know what your purpose is, then you are just not paying attention to what your gut is telling you. It is hushed by what you think are the expectations of others. That needs to stop. You can meditate, or you can just think it through. But the answers to what your purpose is right now, at this time in your life, are within you. Life purpose is too big of a concept. Too vague and too scary to deal with for most of us. But what do you really want? What matters to you the most right now, at this point in your life, at the exact point that you are at? Of course you know the answer. You know yourself. You just don't listen to your gut sometimes. You *have* a purpose. Now let it guide you. Because the truth of the matter is, deep in your gut, you know what matters to you the most. Go with it. The clearer the purpose, the greater the motivation to pursue it.

#46

Solutions May Come from the Most Unexpected People

*"Every great and deep difficulty bears in itself its own solution.
It forces us to change our thinking in order to find it."*
—Niels Bohr

You never know who may become a resource to you and how they can help you. Who may reach out. Who may become a key person under very specific circumstances. How often we rely on those that we shouldn't rely on and disregard the value of people that may become key people for us. You can hear the smartest advice from the most unpredictable people. You can get unpredictable information or help from people who you did not expect much from or count on. Every person around you is valuable. Every person around you counts. Keep your mind open. Keep yourself aligned and on good terms with people who are positive and want your best. Keep your ears open to good information and good advice. In changing our thinking to be resourceful in the way we look for solutions, we must also change our thinking not to disregard off-the-beaten-path people and their ability to help, whether through advice or through action. Always keep this in mind.

#47

Realize Your Limited Knowledge about Other People's Circumstances

"Darkness cannot drive out darkness; only light can do that.
Hate cannot drive out hate; only love can do that."
—Martin Luther King, Jr.

Other than the fact that it is really not our place as human beings to judge other human beings, judging someone causes them to feel attacked. Someone who judges you is not on your team, not your friend and not your ally. They are often perceived as danger in the sense that they criticize who you are and what you do. The general reaction is usually to stay away from them, physically and emotionally. Who wants to be close to someone who judges you? Judging works against good relationships, against teamwork, and leads to much unnecessary hostility.

The reality is that we assume so many things about the people around us and why they do what they do. This is simply because we do not have much information about them. We fill in those gaps of information with our own assumptions and convince ourselves in our own theories, completely forgetting that these theories are in our minds only.

We know everything about ourselves and very little about the people around us. Always remember that there is a lot that you do not know about the person in front of you. Coming up with assumptions about why they do what they do does not really fill in the gaps—it is only an illusion. While asking people questions may give us some information, they may be completely unready to share things with us. We just have to accept and respect the fact that there is so much we do not know.

#48

Look Beyond Your Current Circumstances

"It's not what you look at that matters, it's what you see."
—Henry David Thoreau

The ability to look beyond your current circumstances is the most positive form of a forward-facing approach. It means that you are rising above your current circumstances, and consider them secondary to how great life will be when you improve your circumstances and your situation. By being able to do that, you are giving yourself hope and strength to deal with the everyday struggles of your current situation, because to you at that time, they do not matter as much compared to the future. You look at your current situation but what you see is the future. This is a remarkable position to be in.

The most powerful methodology of getting yourself to that place is continuously envisioning how you see your future in great detail, and then believing with all of your heart that this is the reality that waits for you just around the corner. As you are doing that, stay focused on your goals and work hard on making progress.

#49

Think Outside of the Box

*"Being an entrepreneur means the ability
to think out of the box by putting away
fear of any risk, including financial."*
—Ciputra

One of the problems that many people face in solving their problems is that they see either one solution or two at the most, and when none of those works or seems realistic, they get very discouraged. Outside-the-box thinking allows people to see additional solutions that other people may not have considered. The power of having multiple options gives not only hope but also practical solutions that people can apply and that may work very well in their benefit. The ability to think outside of the box basically means the ability to think of non-traditional solutions. Neuroscientific research indicates that it becomes increasingly difficult to break out of our existing mindsets. Fortunately, however, it is still possible to train our brains to think differently.

To train your brain to think outside of the box, ask yourself this question:

Are there any other solutions that I have not considered? Write down all the possible solutions, even those that seem like a bad idea or an unrealistic one. This is basically a process where you brainstorm with yourself (if you have someone to actually brainstorm with, even better). The reason why you should write everything down is that sometimes a great idea may evolve from a not-so-great idea, just as part of the thought process. Keep writing options and possible plans until you feel that you have hit something that may work. You can then tweak it to the point that it is ready to be followed up on.

#50

No Matter What's on Your Plate, Turn It into Something Good

"The best preparation for tomorrow is doing your best today."
–H. JACKSON BROWN, JR.

The ability to take pain, sorrow. or any kind of negative event in your life and move with it, not from it, in a forward-facing manner by means of helping others and doing good is a remarkable way to deal with pain and suffering. It is the ultimate form of coping in a proactive and positive way. We hope not to have to deal with the most difficult of circumstances and challenges, but what we can learn from those who do and are able to do good and help others rather than dwell on their own pain is a life lesson that we can all implement in our own lives in various ways. If people can grow from sorrow to the point of helping others and doing good, what excuse do we then have not to do that very same thing? Reaching out to others and doing good does not have to be something big; it can also come down to small acts of kindness. We can do what we feel we are capable of doing, reach out in whatever opportunities come our way, but there is no excuse for any of us not to be performing acts of kindness that will help and empower others.

#51

Get out of the Victim Mode

*"I don't do the victim mode, I don't
do blame. I can't bear that."*
—NOMA DUMEZWENI

One big problem a lot of people have is that they slip into thinking of themselves as victims who have little or no control over their lives. This is a state of mind where you feel sorry for yourself, which causes you to get stuck. You have a hard time taking action and experience a great amount of sadness and self-pity.

Feeling like a victim is a matter of a state of mind. Seeing yourself as the victim is often a call for attention and validation, because it causes other people to show you that they are worried about you and try to help out. The worst part of being in a victim mode is the sense that it excuses you from responsibility. Being the victim is a very passive position to be in, and in many causes it becomes an excuse for lack of accountability.

Being in a victim mode also makes you feel that you are right. That the other person is wrong. That you have been wronged. In the subconscious mind, this is a pleasurable feeling: lots of attention, a lack of accountability, and reduced urgency to take action.

In my experience, by just being aware of the benefits that we can derive from victim thinking, it becomes easier for us to say no to that and to choose to take a different path.

It doesn't matter what the situation was or if you indeed have been wronged. What matters is for you to take an approach that will benefit you the most, an empowered approach, a forward-facing approach, an accountable approach. In other words, an approach toward success.

#52

Learn the Power of Getting Along with Anybody

"For good ideas and true innovation, you need human interaction, conflict, argument, debate."
—MARGARET HEFFERMAN

Theodore Roosevelt said, "The most important single ingredient in the formula of success is knowing how to get along with people." Research after research shows how good relationships with the people around us are important for our health, and even for our longevity. Knowing that, it seems that building good and positive relationships with the people around us would become our most sought-after goal. It holds the key to our happiness and health.

And yet we struggle.

While building and nurturing good relationships with some people in our lives may come easy, there will always be those around us who we truly struggle to get along with. This is both at work and at home. We struggle with our spouses, we struggle with our extended families, with our kids, with certain co-workers, our boss, our clients. That struggle is always there. Upsetting us. Taking its toll on us. Leaving us unsure what to do. Saying some things and then regretting them. Not saying other things, and regretting that too.

For many people, the situation of struggling in our relationship with someone comes with our deeming of them as "difficult." As if deeming those people "difficult" gives us some kind of an excuse to try less, or not to try at all.

The reality is that deeming the other as "difficult" is not a reality, even if we can find five, ten, or fifty people who would agree with us. It would still be a matter of opinion, no matter how we look at it. What is difficult here for sure, and that is not a matter of opinion, is our dynamics with that person. Now, while we don't have control over someone being "difficult," in a way, this excuses us from responsibility for our share of improving the relationship and the dynamics. The fact is that we do have control over changing dynamics if we consider them difficult, simply because no matter how you look at it, dynamics take at least two people.

And this is where the key to change truly lies.

Once you have shifted from talking about "difficult people" to talking about "difficult dynamics," here are five things that you can start doing immediately. These tips will help you change the dynamics with someone who you are struggling to get along with. This will lead you toward greater peace of mind and overall improved happiness and health. (It's amazing what a toll stressful relationships take on us. They are truly something you want to avoid or reduce to an absolute minimum):

1. Accept and respect your differences:

Many times, we judge others simply because they think differently. Our notion that the way we see things is the 'right' way is of course completely in our mind. We have to accept the fact that in order to have good relationships with pretty much anyone in our lives, we cannot limit ourselves to having good relationships with only those who agree with us. It is with those who think differently and are substantially different from us where our greatest challenge lies. But, it is also our greatest opportunity. If we teach ourselves to accept and respect diversity of opinions and points of view, we hold the key to more accepting relationships with challenging people in our lives. Keep in mind that feeling judged and unaccepted does not allow for good relationships to grow. This leads us to the next point.

2. Don't judge:

Other than the fact that it is really not our place as human beings to judge other human beings, judging someone causes them to feel attacked. Someone who judges you is not on your team, not your friend and not your ally. They are often perceived as danger in the sense that they criticize who you are and what you do. The general reaction is usually to stay away from them, physically and emotionally. Who wants to be close to someone who judges you? Judging works against good relationships and against teamwork, and leads to much unnecessary hostility.

3. Listen courageously:

I am sure you have heard before that listening attentively to the other person is important. Many of us are so caught up in what we want to say that we neglect to listen to the other. Listening attentively is only half the work. Listening courageously means that you need to be completely open to feedback that the other person has for you. Yes, you may not be as perfect as you like to think, and it takes a lot of courage to accept and listen to that too. Once you are able to do that, though, there is true opportunity for change and growth. Guaranteed.

4. Don't assume:

The reality is that we assume so many things about the people around us and why they do what they do. This is simply because we do not have much information about them. We fill in those gaps of information with our own assumptions and convince ourselves of our own theories, completely forgetting that these theories are in our minds only.

5. Don't handle a heated situation while it is still hot:

Handling interpersonal situations while you are angry is a huge mistake. We are not in full control of our actions and words when we are very angry. We are likely to say and do things that we will regret. "Don't touch the pot when it's hot" is a sentence that I use a lot with my clients. Unless you want to get burned.

Remember, your happiness, health and longevity depend on the quality of your relationships with the people around you. The power is in your hands to change dynamics, improve interactions, and move forward.

#53

Find Your Why

The two most important days are the day you are born and the day you discover your why."
—MARK TWAIN

Your 'Why' is your purpose or belief that pushes you to do what you do. In most cases, you know your why. You know because you know what matters to you the most. If you do not know what matters to you the most, what motivates you, what blows the wind in your sails, you probably have not been listening to your gut. Here are four questions to ask yourself in order to either find out what your why is, or just make sure that you know what it is:

1. What makes you feel the most alive?

Where in your life do you have that sense of feeling the most alive? Where do you feel most needed? Most valuable? This is typically something that is bigger than what you are, and in that sense ties in with who you are and what you care about the most.

2. What are you really good at?

What are your innate strengths? What are the things that you have always been very good at? We tend to be very passionate about places in our lives where we can shine, where we can show how capable we are.

3. Where can you add the most value?

We want to feel that we matter, that we have made a difference, that the value that we bring is recognized. For that reason, we tend to lean toward doing things where we bring the most value. This is where we shine.

4. What is success to you?

At the end of the day, we want to focus on what matters the most to us. We each have an independent and personal definition of what matters to us the most and what success means to us. Problems typically arise when people do not have clarity on what matters to them the most and mix that with the expectations of their parents or society. It is incredibly important for each of us to be able to make that distinctive definition to ourselves.

#54

Being Hopeless Is Not
an Action Plan

*"Keep your face always toward the sunshine,
and shadows will fall behind you."*
—Walt Whitman

Even in the most seemingly hopeless situations, you can find something that you can do to improve your situation. Thinking that there is nothing that you can do is merely a state of mind. Finding what can be done rather than focusing on what cannot be done is an empowering and forward-facing approach that allows for creative and proactive solutions even in the most challenging situations.

With every difficulty, you have two options: you can accept the difficulty and do nothing but express sadness over it, or you can accept the situation just as much but change something in that situation to the point that it will become more manageable. Every situation has two ends to it: you can focus on the bad, or focus on the good. You can focus on what was lost or you can focus on what can be gained. You can focus on the past or focus on the future. All of these are conscious choices that can be made that completely transform not only our perception of the situation, but also our feelings toward it and, as a result, the action that we take, and ultimately the situation itself. If you are in a situation where you tell yourself that there is nothing that you can do, question that statement. Question your perception. Question how you are handling whatever is on your plate. Rather than focusing on what cannot be done, focus on what you can do. Ask yourself: What can I do to make this better? What is within my capabilities? How can I make it better for myself and for others? What you will find, continuously, is that there is always something that you can do.

#55

Keep an Open Mind

"Always keep an open mind and a compassionate heart."
—PHIL JACKSON

Keeping an open mind means first and foremost that we avoid judging other people. Many times we judge others simply because they think differently. Our notion that the way we see things is the 'right' way is, of course, completely in our mind. We have to accept the fact that in order to have good relationships with pretty much anyone in our lives, we cannot limit ourselves to having good relationships with those who agree with us. It is with those who think differently and are substantially different from us that where our greatest challenge lies. But, also our greatest opportunity. If we teach ourselves to accept and respect diversity of opinions and points of view, we hold the key to more accepting relationships with challenging people in our lives. Keep in mind that feeling judged and unaccepted does not allow for good relationships to grow. By the same token, do not assume things about other people. The reality is that we assume so many things about the people around us and why they do what they do. This is simply because we do not have much information about them. We fill in those gaps of information with our own assumptions and convince ourselves in our own theories, completely forgetting that these theories are in our minds only. Keeping an open mind is about acceptance of differences, acceptance of what we do not know about other people, and avoiding arbitrary stories about why they do what they do that are originated in our own minds. By the same token, it means avoiding thinking that the way we live is better than the way others do, that our norms are everyone's norms and more legitimate than others, and that the way we live, dress, vote, raise our kids, or run our job or household is somehow superior to others.

#56

Be Willing to Do Whatever It Takes

"I'll do whatever it takes to win."
–Terrell Owens

D oing whatever it takes is the ultimate form of passionate action when it comes to what matters to us the most. This is where we are most resourceful and use our utmost capabilities in getting ourselves to a certain place in our lives. It also means that we are ready to pay whatever price tag is attached to that place that we want to get to in our lives, and that our strong desire to accomplish that goal goes above and beyond any required effort. If we have to sweat, we sweat; if we have to retake the class, we will retake the class; if we have to walk we walk, and if we have to get up very early, we will wake up before the alarm. When someone says, "I will do whatever it takes," it means that it will get done. The human will is a mysterious muscle. It stretches itself beyond its capabilities when it really wants something and makes up its mind to achieve it, and then in other circumstances, when it doesn't matter to it as much, it becomes rather loose. What human will actually is is the faculty of the mind that selects, at that very time of making a decision, the strongest desire among various desires that are in the mind at that time. Think of the human will as the mechanism of choosing among desires. In that case, it will always choose what matters to you the most. If eating the cake matters to you at that moment more than losing five pounds, you will probably eat the cake. If you have decided to lose five pounds by your sister's wedding date no matter what, you will not touch it. If finishing your degree is something that you are doing to make your parents happy and you do not feel very passionately about it, you will find it very hard to go to class, finish the book, submit the paper. But if it is in your heart and you have decided to graduate no matter what, you will finish the book even at the expense of your sleep, get to class even in the middle of a rainstorm without an umbrella, and submit the paper even if you spend the whole night on it. Perhaps the human will, as mysterious as it sometimes seems, is actually simpler than we think. We succeed in what matters to us the most.

#57

Learn to Delegate

"From a young age, I learned to focus on things I was good at and delegate to others what I was not good at."
—RICHARD BRANSON

The idea of learning to delegate is closely connected to two other ideas that are of extreme importance when it comes to hitting the Change button in our lives. One is the ability to do teamwork, and the other is the management of our ego. The ability to do teamwork, which is essentially the ability to work well with others, is the ultimate form of being able to get along well with others and increase your power to produce work by joining forces with them. In every change-based situation, whether a company change or a change that an individual is initiating in their own life, there is always the need for the support of others in the form of teamwork. Without teamwork with people around you, it will be very hard for you to make the progress that you are looking to make.

That brings us to the second concept of management of the ego. Many times, people have the glorious idea that they are some kind of superman or superwoman and can do it all completely by themselves without support from others and without teamwork with others. This is a recipe for extreme difficulty and reduced chances of success, because we need the people around us so that we can accomplish our goals. Your success is not an ego-based ride about you being above the need for others' help. Your success is about taking your life to the next level, and it is closely linked with your ability to work well with others in your life—your family, friends, spouse, coworkers, colleagues. Take a realistic look at what needs to be done this week or this month in order for you to accomplish your goals. What can you delegate? Who can help you? What would that delegation enable you to do? How can you make this delegation happen? What needs to happen in order for it to take place? Let the people around you know how much they matter, how much you need them in order to accomplish your goals. Empower them and thank them. See what you can do in return for them. And every time you look at your goals, ask yourself: What can I delegate to make sure that everything gets done? What room and space does it give me to accomplish more or accomplish my goals faster?

#58

Remember to Be Grateful

"Feeling gratitude and not expressing it is like
wrapping a present and not giving it."
—WILLIAM ARTHUR WARD

The power of gratitude goes above and beyond the ability to appreciate what we have. It digs deep into the power of attitude, and that's where its greatest merits are. The basic principle of it all is that the more we focus on something, the more of it we will see in our lives. The more we focus on problems, the more problems we are likely to experience. The more we focus on success, the more success we are going to see. Gratitude focuses us on what is good. It focuses on what we have and on what we can work with. In that sense, it causes us to become more powerful and more capable, because we then realize not where our problems and challenges are, but where our strengths and capabilities are. As a result, we feel happier with our lives and we are able to accomplish way over what we thought was possible. Gratitude, then, is a matter of focus and perspective. If you are having a hard time expressing gratitude, you are having a hard time with your attitude toward life and with your perspective, your view, of the situation. As yourself: What can I be thankful for? What good is there in my life? The fact that you are alive is something to be very thankful for. If you have people that care about you, it is something to be very thankful for. Even your challenges and problems are something to be thankful for because there is a lesson and growth potential in each and every one of them. We just take things for granted, things that are actually not trivial at all like life and people and a roof over our head, our freedom and our opportunities. The scientific benefits of changing your attitude to a gratitude attitude are incredible. You will feel better, sleep better, be kinder and more compassionate, and even your immune system will become stronger. We are designed to feel positive feelings of gratitude—it is good for us, good for our relationships with others, and good for our health, and contributes to our success.

#59

Choose to Make a Difference

"Each of us can make a difference.
Together we can make a change."
—Barbara Mikulski

Making a difference is about tying your goals into goals that are greater than your individual self. This may be anything from providing a better life for your family to helping humanity, wherever your heart is and whatever is most important to you at this point in time. The important thing is to realize your incredible power to help others and make a difference in other people's lives. By helping others and making a difference, you are also helping yourself. Here are four scientific benefits that prove that helping others actually helps you:

1. Helping others helps you live longer:

Studies indicate that acts of kindness toward others boost your health in a way that may impact your longevity. They boost your immune system, help eliminate or reduce depression, help with social life regulation, and increase people's long-term health.

2. Helping others makes you feel happier:

Acts of kindness and giving back to the community make people happier because they have an increased sense of value, an increased sense of purpose, and are getting a mental boost by being provided with the neurochemical sense of reward as a result of their volunteer work.

3. Helping others helps with chronic pain:

Studies have shown that people that suffered from chronic pain experienced reduced symptoms as a result of volunteer work. The assumption is that the sense of feeling good about their volunteer work helped pain by releasing oxytocin to the blood.

4. Helping others lowers blood pressure:

Research has shown that individuals, and particularly older individuals, who volunteered at least 200 hours annually had significantly decreased risk of hypertension as a result of increased social activity and overall sense of happiness and satisfaction

#60

Forgive and Move On

"The weak can never forgive.
Forgiveness is the attribute of the strong."
—MAHATMA GANDHI

Forgiveness is about the self before it is about others. When we forgive others, we do it first and foremost for ourselves. The reason is that we want to have a forward-facing life, a future-oriented attitude, and we cannot do that until we forgive, which keeps us deeply rooted, or in other words, deeply stuck, in the past. In that sense, forgiveness sets you free. It sets you free from the pain over something that is in the past and cannot be changed, it sets you free from anger and negative feelings, and it sets you free to move on. Until you forgive, you are a prisoner of your anger and hurt. Once we forgive, we are able to grow and nourish ourselves. Often we find over time that the situation that we were once so angry and unforgiving about is far more complex than we had realized. We have incredible expertise in our own life circumstances—how we were wronged, how much we didn't deserve it, how unfair it was—but we do not know much about the life circumstances of the other. Why they did what they did. What caused them to act the way they have acted. What their circumstances were. Forgiveness is the realization that there is much that we do not know. The realization that we do not put ourselves in a judgement position of another human being for first and foremost the reason of lack of knowledge about the complex life circumstances that have led them to a certain action. Many times, because we do not have

118

that knowledge, we make up for that gap in our minds by just making up information. We might say: She did that because she does not love and respect me, or, He did that because he cares only about himself. We understand that this is just us telling ourselves the story of what we think the circumstances were that led to a certain incident or series of incidents, we do not have the full information and so there is a lot that we do not know. How much do you really know about your parents? How much do you really know about the people you work with? Not much. Practice forgiveness not just as a means of freedom, but also as a means of humility and human connectedness. It is the ultimate form of being the best person that you can become.

#61

Adopt a Full Glass Mentality

"Pessimism leads to weakness, optimism to power."
–WILLIAM JAMES

Adopting a full glass mentality is a matter of perspective and attitude. In every situation, you can find polarized lenses to look at the situation from completely different angles. You can look at a situation and think how horrible and difficult it is, but you can always, no matter what the situation is, find something positive to say or think about it. I often think that having a full glass perspective or an empty glass perspective are not necessarily the only possible perspectives, because having a glass by itself already presents an opportunity. Train your mind to see the good in every situation. Always say to yourself: There is good in every situation. Where do I see the good in this and how can I be thankful for it? You will find that over time, it will become increasingly easier for you to see the good. It is not necessarily a question of personality. Perspective is also something that you can train yourself at, and you will find it extremely helpful in helping you work through challenging situations. This is because when you see the good, the challenge is not as intimidating and the difficulties are not as burdening.

Here is a simple method to train your brain to have a full glass mentality:

1. Pay attention to the people who you are with. If you are around negative people that spread negative, empty glass energy, you

may want to reconsider your company. Optimism, as much as pessimism, is contagious.

2. Imagine the worst-case scenario. Could things have been worse for you? Now look at your current situation. This will help you with perspective.

3. Remind yourself of the privilege of choice. Ask yourself: What choice can I make right now to make myself feel better? Be thankful for having that choice and for being able to be kind to yourself. Once you do that for yourself, you will feel better, and you are far more likely to have the room to take a more optimistic look at the situation that you are dealing with.

#62

Control Your Own Destiny

"Control your own destiny or someone else will,"
—Jack Welch

The most difficult mental state to be in is the sense of being helpless. Adulthood is about taking charge, being in charge and making choices. When we feel powerless, we become hopeless, and these two feelings, feeling powerless and feeling hopeless, feed off of each other. The good news is that both of these feelings are not only completely subjective but also a matter of choice, and for those reasons, can be quickly turned around with our power of inner perspective and personal will. I have worked for a long time with people in difficult divorce situations and learned that the hardest place to be in in a situation of divorce is when people feel that the situation of divorce is imposed on them and they do not have the power to choose if they want to be married or separated. The truth of the matter is that in every situation you have the power to choose. You can always choose you reaction, and by making certain choices in terms of your reactions, you can completely transform the situation. When you let others decide for you, or control and manage the situation for you, because you feel too overwhelmed or feel that you do not have the knowledge or the tools to make the necessary decisions, you have just given up on the most fundamental human privilege: the privilege of choice. No matter what situation you are dealing with, always tell yourself: I am so grateful for my privilege of choosing. I can choose my reaction. I have options. I am going to weigh my options and I am going to take charge of my life. Never accept any situation as a given. Always ask yourself these questions:

- What am I avoiding?
- Why am I avoiding it?
- How can I stop avoiding it?
- What are my priorities?
- What matters to me the most?
- What can I change right now in order to promote what matters to me the most?
- What steps can I take today, tomorrow, this week?

#63

Choose to Be Happy

When you experience pain and negative feelings, the idea that you can choose to be happy seem distant and impossible. The truth of the matter is that choosing to be happy is a question of perspective. We can reset our perspective to focus on the good in our lives and on what we are thankful for, to look at our challenges as opportunities for growth and embrace them. Research indicates that our overall mood and sense of emotional well-being is partially determined by genetics and upbringing, but roughly 40% of it is within our control, which is a substantial potential for choice and change. A large body of psychological research shows that happiness is a conscious choice that people can make. People can change their lives and their experience of life by changing their attitude, or in other words, choosing to be happy by focusing on their attitude rather than on their circumstances. You will not become happier when you have more money, find the house of your dreams, buy the car of your dreams, or meet the spouse of your dreams. Each of these events are nice and happy events and may provide you with temporary feelings of happiness and satisfaction, but they will not provide you with an ongoing sense of happiness. What will provide you with an ongoing sense of happiness is the conscious choice that you can make to be happy, positive, and grateful. Here are three ways to support your choice to be happy in a way that is independent of your circumstances. In other words, it is not the car you drive that determines if you are happy, it is your attitude:

1. When something positive happens, dwell on it:

Because we tend to suffer from Negativity Bias, which means that we give more attention to negative events than to positive ones, make a conscious choice to dwell on and highlight positive things that have happened to you today or recently. This counters the brain's bias and increases your sense of happiness.

2. Smile:

Do not underestimate the importance and impact of something as simple as your smile. Research shows that smiling is contagious and spreads positive energy. When you smile, people smile back at you, and it boosts your happiness. Give it a try and see how it impacts your day.

3. Let yourself be happy:

Bronnie Ware, a palliative care nurse who spent years working with elderly people on their deathbeds, noticed a common theme that came up repeatedly among her patients at the end of their lives: They regretted not "letting" themselves be happy.

Ware, the author of *The Top Five Regrets of the Dying*, wrote in a Huffington Post blog:

> *Many did not realize until the end that happiness is a choice. They had stayed stuck in old patterns and habits. The so-called 'comfort' of familiarity overflowed into their emotions, as well as their physical lives. Fear of change had them pretending to others, and to their selves, that they were content. When deep within, they longed to laugh properly and have silliness in their life again...Life is a choice. It is YOUR life. Choose consciously, choose wisely, choose honestly. Choose happiness.*

#64

Never Be Too Proud to Seek Help

"Humble people ask for help."
—JOYCE MEYER

The ability to know when to ask for help is critical to people's ability to transform their lives. This may come in the form of a need for professional help from a therapist or a psychologist to overcome emotional obstacles, this may come in the form of seeking corporate or executive coaching or other means of mentoring and support, or this may come in the form of consulting with others. In any form, the ability to seek the help and advice of another person, whatever the format or need may be, is often the key to people's ability to break barriers in their lives. This requires humility, because this is where you acknowledge your limitations and realize your need for the support of another person in order to overcome them. It is a point where humility, self-realization, and determination come together for the purpose of overcoming obstacles. I must say, the refusal to get help must be seen in that respect as the opposite. It is a form of arrogance that often comes with a high price tag. People who refuse to get help are willing to pay the price as long as their vulnerability is not exposed and does not cause them any sense of embarrassment or discomfort. It is also an expression of lack of trust in others.

The truth of the matter is that asking for help does not weaken your power, it boosts it. The challenge is often in taking the first step. Make it your goal to create the system of people who will help you, and see it as teamwork toward your goals rather than as a sign of weakness. Once you take that first step and ask for help, you will find that people are happy to help you, and that you have a sense of relief and empowerment. This is not you giving up face or power. This is you taking control and managing your life in way that will allow you to remove obstacles and take your life to the next level.

#65

Take Risks

*"Only those who will risk going too far can
possibly find out how far one can go."*
–T.S ELIOT

Change, in itself, is a form of risk. One of the most common illusions that we have is that if we are not changing things, we are avoiding risk. One of the most common thought fallacies is the Conservation Bias. The Conservation Bias is the misconception that the right approach to risk is to eliminate or minimize it. In reality, risk is a vital and absolutely necessary part of life. When we embrace the idea of doing nothing rather than embracing risk, we end up missing out on opportunities. Jim Rohn said once that the best way to avoid risk is to place yourself in a bubble inside your home and live your life there. Would you be 100% safe? No. Are you likely to be safer from a statistical standpoint? Probably, but is that the life you choose to have? Is that a life worth living? Here are three questions that you should ask yourself regarding the risk that you are facing:

1. How do I define the risk?
2. What is the worst-case scenario?
3. How can I mitigate the risk?
4. What is my gut telling me to do?

While risk is an essential step toward change and success, the most important tool to mitigate it is to avoid impulsive decisions. Define to yourself clearly what the risk is, look the worst-case scenario straight in the eye, check how to mitigate the risk, and then, if you decide to go for it, just go for it.

#66

It's All about Perseverance

*"Perseverance is the hard work you do after you get
tired doing the hard work you already did."*
—NEWT GINGRICH

Perseverance is the ability to do something in spite of difficulty or delay in achieving what we want. It is our ability to recover from failure, get up, and either continue on our path or find a new one. It keeps us immune to a sense of humiliation, disappointment, and discouragement, and is considered to be the most important factor in people's ability to create a change in their lives and take them to the next level, no matter what their circumstances are and what difficulties they face. Here are the four most important factors that contribute to perseverance. Perseverance is a winning combination of positive attitude and active choices.

Positive Attitude: A positive attitude is a driving force. It is the desire to move forward, to persevere when there are supposedly legitimate reasons to quit, to retreat in the face of change and hardship. It is the choice not only to see the good but to envision and then follow up on potential.

Active Choices: Perseverance is active decisive making in spite and in the face of hardship and difficulty. It is the choice to be active and decisive rather than passive and indecisive. While not all decisions and choices are guaranteed to be the best, indecisiveness and lack of action are the worst choice when dealing with hardship and challenge.

Determination and persistence in the form of positive attitude, in envisioning the potential and making active choices to promote your way there, are what determine your success in spite of all circumstances and in the face of all challenges.

#67

Never Underestimate the
Power of Planning

*"All you need is the plan, the road map and the
courage to press on to your destination."*
—EARL NIGHTINGALE

Research shows that only 3% of all adult citizens in the United States take the time and effort to plan for the future. Yet, those 3% accomplish five to ten times more in their lifetimes than do the other 97%. It is a shame, but most people spend more time planning their vacations than they do planning their lives. Individuals who take the time to determine, with clarity, what they want to achieve in life are much more likely to accomplish their goals & objectives than those who leave their lives to chance. Planning your goals and your way of accomplishing them should not take more than five minutes a day. I find it hard to believe, and I am sure that you will agree with me, that you do not have five minutes a day to invest in your future, when research and data show so clearly that planning your way toward your goals is critical and essential to your success. To plan easily, not having to spend more than five minutes a day on it, here is a simple method. Every weekend, before you start your week, list at least five things that you absolutely have to accomplish that week. Make your plan as specific as possible and assign a deadline (a day of the week) for each task. If you need to make a certain call by Monday, write it for Monday. If you need to sign up for a certain class or finish a certain assignment by Thursday, write it for that day. Your list should not include your everyday chores, but only things that go beyond your daily chores, and should align completely with your goals. This list should be short, uncomplicated, and ready to go by Sunday Monday. Start every day by reviewing what needs to be done for that day and cross it out as you go. If you did not do something by the designated deadline, move it forward to another day. In doing that, you are making the steps toward your goals concrete and tangible and making sure that you are progressing toward your goals in a continuous manner.

#68

Tune the Noise Out

"It is during our darkest moments that
we must focus to see the light."
—ARISTOTLE

When we talk about the need to tune the noise out, we have to define what that noise it, and why is it so important to tune it out. Inherently, we know deep in our gut what we want, what matters to us the most, and why we want it. If we do not know it yet, we will find sooner or later in our life journey what matters to us the most and why. Many times, the reason why we are not tuned in with that is that our mind is filled with noise. This includes other people's expectations of us (or what we think are their expectations of us), comparing ourselves to others, self-doubt, and lack of self-confidence and anxious feelings as a result. Tuning all of these out is essential for us so that we can focus on what matters to us the most rather than on running around in circles trying to please others or gain their approval. Here are three things that you should tell yourself every day, continuously, in order to tune the noise of expectations and lack of self-confidence out:

1. I am good enough in whatever I do, and I improve and grow every day.
2. The worst form of betrayal is self-betrayal. I am loyal to myself and to what is the right choice for me.

3. I will be the very best person that I can be in whatever I do for myself and for those in my life that matter to me the most.

Your life matters. Your choices matter. You determine the course of your life.

#69

Be Willing to Change

*"Everyone thinks of changing
the world, but no one thinks
of changing himself."*
–Leo Tolstoy

People's willingness to change is their ability to commit themselves to a process that challenges their existing attitudes. In many cases, people dread change. Here are the four main psychological reasons for people's resistance to change:

Change requires effort:

It requires us to work harder on our focus and awareness. It requires us to process new information. It is much easier and more convenient to do more of the same, more of the familiar and known, simply because it requires less mental effort.

What you can do—
Write everything down. It will help you get a concrete feeling in terms of what you are looking to accomplish and what needs to get done and will provide you with a concrete and less intimidating plan, broken into smaller tasks.

Change causes fear of the unknown:

We know what life looks like now, but what would life look like after we change some significant things in our life? If we feel that the risks involving the change are too great or too unknown to us, we are likely to resist it. Will we still be loved? Will we be able to stand up to the challenge? Will we lose something or some things that we consider to be dear to our heart?

What you can do—
Write down the risks vs. the gains. The answer will speak to you from the paper that you have written your risks and gains on.

We dread the Ripple Effect:

The same way that we toss a pebble into a pond and it creates ripples, change causes other changes beyond the actual concrete change itself. Because we do not know what to expect with the Ripple Effect, we dread other changes that may happen, and we worry about their impact.

What you can do—
Focus yourself on the gains from the change that you are looking to create, and envision your success. Tell yourself that if the Ripple Effect happens, you'll just deal with it as it comes, and that it will not necessarily matter to you as much as it seems like it will right now.

The Weight of the past:

If we have tried to change things in the past but were not successful, whether in the same area or in completely different areas, or if we have witnessed key figures in our lives such as our parents, siblings, or close friends not handling change in a successful manner, it may impact our level or anxiety in dealing with change in a negative manner.

What you can do—
Decide that you are on a new path. You are not your parents. You are not your siblings, and you are not anybody else. You are on your own path, and the power is in your hands. Their journey is their journey. This one is yours.

#70

Make Success Your Mindset

If you are looking for ways to develop a success mindset, understand that success is not a single accomplishment or achievement, it is a way of life and a mindset change. When you have a success mindset, you are able to change the course of your life for the best on multiple levels simply because you think, make decisions, and manage your life differently. To master success as a mindset, you need to first make sure that you are doing something that you love to do. You are far more likely to be successful in doing something that you love so much and feel so passionate about that you do not feel like you are working, you feel like you are in the process of becoming better and improving your ability and skills in order to do what you feel passionate about. If you are at a job that you hate, doing something that you do not like or care for, and need your job in order to pay your bills or for other financial or practical reasons, stick with it, but alongside it start carving the way to what you feel matters to you the most, what you feel passionate about and where you feel you can excel and make the most impact. It may take you some time to carve the way, but keep at it until you can make that shift. Make it your goal and your plan to carve the way to that shift, and you will succeed. Those who love what they do are far more likely not only to succeed but also to deal with setbacks and failures better.

Set goals for yourself, create a plan, and follow up on that strategy. Think every day what short-term goals you can accomplish that day that will align with your long-term goals, and keep crossing them off your list. Keep yourself disciplined in as many areas of your life as possible, because discipline in one area of life tends to impact others. Most importantly, tell yourself that you are capable, resilient, and powerful, and block negativity and disbelievers from your immediate environment.

#71

Don't Say "I Can't"

"Don't let what you cannot do interfere with what you can do."
–John Wooden

O ur language and the things we say impact our actions and the choices that we make. You become not only what you repeatedly think but also what you repeatedly say. We need to be mindful in the words we choose, in the phrases we incorporate into our daily lives, because they have tremendous impact on our subconscious mind and, as a result, on our behavior choices. Here are five phrases to take out of your daily jargon:

1. "It's not fair."

Expecting things to be fair is very naïve and immature. We all know that life is not fair, so it doesn't make you look very good when you state that you have an expectation that is childish to begin with. You can refer to facts that you consider to be something that needs to be changed and suggest a concrete change instead. Something along the lines of: I have a suggestion of how we can perhaps divide the work between us in a different way.

2. "I'm going to ask a stupid question" or "This may be silly."

When you say something like that, you are completely diminishing yourself not only in the eyes of the other person, but also in the way you position yourself in your own mind. Now you are at the mercy of the other person to grant you the much desirable, "There are no stupid questions." If you have a question that needs to be asked, just ask it. There is no need to diminish yourself prior to asking the question.

3. "This will only take a minute."

When you use the expression "This will only take a minute," you are diminishing the value of any time that is spent with you. You are basically positioning yourself in a place where the other person's time is more valuable and you are nothing but an intruder with little value to offer. Drop that language.

4. "It's not my fault."

This is a defensive expression and a clumsy attempt at excusing yourself from responsibility. The whole language of blame, whether of the world's order (as in "It's not fair"), of the other, or of yourself, is far from constructive. See where you can take responsibility and own up to it. Speak in terms of responsibility and accountability, and avoid language of fault and blame.

5. "I can't."

Don't focus on what you can't do. Always speak of what you can do within a certain situation. How can you help? What can you do? How can you contribute? This is not a question of ability. This is a question of what you put the focus on.

#72

Guard Your Health

*"I believe that the greatest gift that you can give
your family and the world is a healthy you."*
—JOYCE MEYER

Guarding your health and keeping yourself healthy has a lot to do with your overall success. This is because one discipline leads to another. When you are disciplined in the way you choose your food, when you are keeping yourself disciplined as far as your fitness, your checkups, and your overall health, you are probably disciplined in other areas of your life as well. If you think about it, it is not very likely for someone to be very disciplined in one area of their lives, and then extremely disciplined in another. Discipline creates stability and fosters structure, which are both essential to success. If you analyze the most successful people, they are very disciplined in how they manage their lives. Discipline promotes good human behavior and good choices. We will always be tempted to waste time, do nothing, do less, make excuses. Discipline keeps us consistent and accountable and we need it for health, wealth, and success, and for the overall way in which we carry ourselves and manage our lives. You need to be at your best health in order to be your best self. You need to go the extra mile in every area of your life in order to be successful. Keep this in mind: everything counts. The way you carry yourself. The way you dress. The way you talk. The way you treat others. The way you handle crises. The way you take care of your health and wellness, physically and emotionally. Your choices matter.

All of your choices. Your financial choices. Your behavior choices. Your words. Your actions. Your health and wellness choices. Your financial choices. All of these are interrelated. When you take care of your health, you tell yourself: I love myself enough to take care of myself. I love myself enough to be disciplined and mindful in my choices. Everything matters. You matter.

#73

Never Lose Hope

"We must accept finite disappointment, but never lose infinite hope."
—MARTIN LUTHER KING, JR.

N ever losing hope is easier said than done. When obstacles and challenges are difficult to tackle, you may find yourself questioning if you can overcome, if you can persevere, if you can make it happen. The main challenge in life is that we never know what is around the corner for us. We never know how close we are to breakthrough, and if things will turn out better for us the next day. Not losing hope is greater than just keeping at a task. Not losing hope means not losing the essence of what we are here for. We need hope. We need to dream. We need hope, because hope gives us purpose. How are we then to do that? How do we not lose hope even in the darkest of times? Here are the three things to keep in mind when you almost lose hope. These are the three most important things to remind yourself.

Number One:

When you are in a difficult time, you should remember: Why do you do what you do? What difference can you make in your life or in the lives of your loved ones if you succeed? Remembering your *why* gives you the push to keep going. It is your why that will push you forward. As Viktor Frankl said: *"Those who have a 'why' to live, can bear with almost any 'how.'"*

Number Two: What CAN you be thankful for?

The second way that you can avoid losing hope in life is to think of things that you *do* have. Things that are ok. Things that you can be thankful for. They may be small, they may be bigger, but this will help you adjust your perspective. Many times, we compare ourselves to those in life that we feel are luckier than us and have more than us. Most of all, be thankful for your ability to change your attitude and mindset toward the situation. This is where your greatest power lies.

Number Three: Take care of yourself, and only then look for solutions.

Be kind to yourself, reach out to your support system, make sure that you ate, that you showered, that you do not look for a solution when you are at a high level of distress. Understand that when you are at a high level of distress, your thinking capabilities and resourcefulness are compromised. You are likely to be more impulsive, and your strategizing abilities are at their lowest point. When you are calm, you can think more clearly and strategize better. The solution may not come to your mind today. It may come to your mind tomorrow. Give yourself the time to regroup. There is a reason for it: to find the inner strength you need to be at your best, and you cannot be at your best when you are at a very high level of distress.

#74

Rejection Is a Part of Pushing Forward

*"Every candle that gets lit in the dark room must feel a little
rejection from the darkness around it, but the last thing I want from
those that hold a different world view to me is to accept me."*
—KIRK CAMERON

The most fascinating thing about rejection is that it actually served a vital function in our evolutionary past. In our hunter/gatherer past, being rejected from our tribes basically meant a death sentence, because there was no way for an individual to survive on their own. Psychologists assume that the brain developed an early warning system to alert us when we were at risk for being rejected. This explains the magnitude of the distress, and many of the physical symptoms that usually accompany it. Because in modern life, rejection is an essential part of trying, daring, and subsequently progressing, which is the essence of change. We need to learn to cope with it in spite of the high-level distress it causes us. Here are the four most important strategies for coping with rejection and moving forward:

1. Remind yourself that rejection is a sign that you are pushing your limits.

Being rejected means that you are living your life to the fullest. You know that it will happen, you know that it is something to deal with, and you know that you have success in other ways in your life to help you balance it out. And if you still do not have it, you are working toward it. Remember this: people who rarely or never get rejected live far into their comfort zones. They are not pushing themselves to their limits, and they are not challenging themselves in any way. This is not living life to the fullest. This is living in your comfort zone and compromising to the fullest.

2. Be kind to yourself.

Don't give yourself a hard time over the circumstances that led to your rejection. Negative self-talk is really the worst form of abuse. Talk to yourself as if you were your best friend. What would you tell your best friend if it happened to them?

3. Rejection does not define you.

Rejection is a single incident. Even if it is a series of incidents, it is likely to be a series of incidents in one area of your life. Do not make it bigger than it is, and certainly do not let it define you. If one company turns you down after a job interview, it does not mean that you are incompetent. If you asked someone out and they refused, it does not mean that you are not a loveable person. Keep things in perspective.

4. Learn from rejection.

Many times, rejection is the best teacher. If we take that rejection for what it is, and do not make it bigger than it actually is, we can look at it and learn from it. What can we do better next time? Where do we need to improve the way we manage the situation? You just practiced. You just got a lesson. On to better things and better outcomes.

#75

Guard Your Thoughts

"You become what you think about."
—Napoleon Hill

The way we process information, the way we interpret reality (or in other words, our thoughts) determines all of our subsequent actions. To change your life, to hit the Change button without changing the way you perceive yourself, is hardly possible. The way you perceive yourself is what will determine all of your actions. If you perceive yourself as confident, powerful, capable, and resourceful, you will act accordingly. If you perceive yourself as someone who always fails or someone who is not very capable, you are likely to become one of those people who fail multiple times in whatever they do. In that respect, your thoughts have complete control over your reality. What this means is that you need to be very aware of what you are thinking. And particularly: What are you thinking about yourself? What you are thinking about yourself is greatly shaped by key figures in your life, mostly from your childhood: your parents, your teachers, etc. If you have someone who believed in you, who thought that you were very capable, it surely impacted your entire life. If you were told that you were no good, one of two things must have happened: it either made you very angry, and you are spending your life in an effort to prove that wrong by accumulating success, or you bought into that narrative in your thoughts and somehow conducted your life accordingly. The good news is that you can choose your thoughts. Your thoughts are not a part of you, as impactful as they may be. They are external to you. If a thought comes to your mind that you feel is not good for your success, something negative that may ruin things for you, remind yourself that this thought is external to you. It is just a thought. Ask yourself: Where did it come from? Who put that thought into my head? And then brush it off, and replace it with a thought of your choosing. Because thoughts can be very persistent—especially if we are used to thinking thoughts similar to them for many years, the negative thoughts will try to find their way back into your mind. Reject them and repeat to yourself your alternative uplifting thought over and over again, like a mantra.

#76

Failure Is Your Best Teacher

"You have to be able to accept
failure to get better."
—LEBRON JAMES

The fact that we know that we all win and we all lose and that failure is a part of our journey toward change is not enough. The amount of learning and information you get from a failure depends on how you approach and analyze it. Failure can also happen without any learning, and that is one waste of a failure. Failure is such a valuable lesson because it shows you what happens when you manage things one way, so that you can learn to manage them in another. For that reason, the analysis of your failure is your most important force for moving forward from it. Here are three important questions to ask yourself when you look at something that you have failed at. Remember these, and use them every time you fail, as part of your moving forward to success:

1. Was I well prepared?

Be specific with yourself so that you can get the full picture. How were you prepared? What was good about the way you prepared? Was there anything lacking in your preparation? Would you prepare differently in retrospect? How? What are three things that you would do differently in terms of preparation?

2. Did I do a good job?

Be specific here as well. Saying to yourself that you did a good job or didn't do a good job is not enough for you to learn from. Name three ways in which you did an excellent job. Name three things that were not so good. How good was your job on a scale from

3. What was within my control, and what wasn't?

Name three things that were within your control in managing the situation. How did you handle them? Name three things that were not within your control. Accept what you cannot control, and define to yourself in one sentence what the impact was of what you could not control in the situation.

#77

Clear Goals Will Help You
Overcome Adversity

"Set your goals high, and don't
stop until you get there."
–Bo Jackson

One of the main problems for most people is that they do not know how to set goals. They think that they are setting goals, but what they are actually doing is expressing aspirations. Think of your goals as the destinations that you put into your life's GPS. Would your GPS be able to find its way to your desired destination if it is unclear on what this destination is? Not a chance. How will you then be able to accomplish your goals if you do not define them to yourself clearly enough?

A goal that is unclear:
I want to lose some weight.

A clearly defined goal:
I want to lose 10 pounds by Christmas.

A goal that is unclear:
I want to make more money.

A clearly defined goal:
I want to increase my income by 25% by the end of this year.

You see the difference? The difference is threefold: a clearly defined goal states a well-defined action by a well-defined deadline in a clear manner.

Ask yourself these three simple questions in order to define your goals clearly:

- What specifically do I want to accomplish?
- By when?
- How much?

#78

Create New Habits Rather Than Fighting Your Old Ones

"We are what we repeatedly do. Excellence, then, is not an act but a habit."
—WILL DURANT

Because our brain conserves so much of our overall energy (20%), we cannot trust it to make decisions that will be good for us and that will promote change in our lives. One of the most common cognitive biases (biases in our mind in terms of our subjective perception of reality) is the Status Quo bias. This is where our brain prefers to avoid change and all the effort that comes with it: processing new information, taking new decisions, etc. The brain really prefers to be on autopilot, which is why habits form most of our behavior. To overcome this, and to be able to create significant changes in our lives, we need to think in terms of replacing old and undesirable habits with new and desirable ones. This way, we put the brain on autopilot, but on a new route. It takes anywhere from under a month to close to two months for a new habit to be formed, and you have to look at that timeframe as the time where you do not take this new habit for granted, where you are getting very busy reinforcing it over and over again by keeping yourself accountable and on track. The best way to do that is to take three simple steps:

1. Write down to yourself what that new habit is. Be brief, clear, and as specific as you possibly can.

CAN WE **CHANGE** FOR A **CHANGE?**

2. Keep the written habit in a visible place and check off the days next to it until you reach two months.

3. Keep yourself accountable by starting your count over every time you slack.

#79

Don't Expect Immediate Results

"It takes 20 years to make an overnight success."
—EDDIE CANTOR

There is a growing culture of impatience. The Pew Research Center's Internet & American Life Project sums up a recent study about people under the age of 35 and the dangers of their hyper-connected lives with what sounds like a prescription drug warning: "Negative effects include a need for instant gratification and loss of patience."

Janakiraman conducted a 2011 study called, "The Psychology of Decisions to Abandon Waits for Service." Subjects were made to wait for downloads and kept on hold as they waited for help from a call center. As predicted, many test subjects who were forced to wait abandoned the process.

"It's why you have people at Disney World paying for a pass so they don't have to wait in line," he added. "You have people who don't mind paying for things like same-day delivery."

Expecting immediate and unrealistic results sets many people up for failure. When you set a goal, and you set a realistic timeline for yourself, you know, consciously, that you are setting a timeline that is both realistic and challenging. The notion that you will eat healthy for a few days and everyone will notice a remarkable change is not a good way to go about a change. Tell yourself over and over again: This is not a one-time operation. This is a lifestyle. This is how I do things. This will give you a sense of perspective and patience in a rapidly moving, social-media saturated, unrealistic social environment in the age that we all live in.

#80

Break the Cycles That You Don't Like:

*"Life and death are illusions. We are in a
constant state of transformation."*
—Alejandro Gonzalez Inarritu

Behavior patterns, cycles, and choices turn to repeat themselves. We tend to repeat the same behavior over and over again, and then with increased intensity, because we get very frustrated, just to end up getting the same result. There are three steps to breaking a behavior pattern that you can easily follow. Keep in mind that the first step, identifying the pattern, is the key one. Often, we do not see our own behavior patterns and the great similarity between things that happen to us that are supposedly very different—different people, different circumstances, different details—but actually carry very similar characteristics. Here are the three steps for breaking behavior patterns:

1. Identify Your Patterns:

It is hard to identify our own patterns. It is much easier to see other people's behavior patterns than to see our own. What happens to people in therapy is that they tell the therapist their life stories and through the storytelling, with some guiding questions, become aware of their behavior and life patterns. You can go to therapy, talk to a friend, or just tell yourself or write to yourself what your life story is. Ask yourself: Did something similar happen to me before? What were my other relationships like? What were my other jobs like? What happened to me in similar cases? You need to become mindful by listening to what you are saying, by listening to yourself. The patterns will emerge right out of your story.

2. Define your pattern using the One Sentence Strategy.

The One Sentence Strategy is a strategy where you define to yourself something that is actually quite complex, in one sentence. You do that in order to make sure that it is defined clearly and that you gain a sharp and clear understanding of the behavior pattern that you are dealing with.

3. Define your Actionable Change.

Your Actionable Change is an alternative behavior pattern that you are now choosing in a mindful manner in order to replace a behavior pattern that you have identified as a negative one in your life. This is where you identify a behavior pattern that hurts your life, reject it, and decide in a concrete and clear manner how to act differently going forward.

#81

Reach High and Then Higher

"Don't limit yourself to the skies when there is a whole galaxy out there."
—BIANCA FRAZIER

S uccess breeds success and you grow with it. What you are setting as your goals at a given time and based on specific circumstances may grow and change with you over time. Think of it as climbing a ladder.

Before you start climbing the ladder, your goal is setting your foot on the first or second step. You do not think about the eighth of eleventh step in the ladder. You progress as you go. None of the goals you set for yourself are permanent. They grow and change with you as you go. You adjust them up as you climb the ladder. As you accumulate success, you set your goal to succeed more. If you had managed to do something remarkable, you may want to reach out to others and help them do the same. You may have not thought about it before you did the remarkable thing that you did.

#82

Train Yourself to Listen

"In English you have this wonderful difference between listening and hearing, and that you can hear without listening, and you can listen and not hear."
—Daniel Barenboim

The art of listening to another is a wonderful tool. It is not only the right thing to do but also a very smart thing to do. It is an important skill to know how to give another human being your undivided attention. In doing that, you tell them without words how much they matter. On the contrary, when you are distracted and do not give the other person your undivided attention, you actually tell them without words that they really do not matter to you much. Another important benefit of truly listening to another person has to do with collecting valuable information. There is a lot of information that will come your way when you truly listen to another person. There are details they are telling you that can put a bigger picture together. There is a lot of information in their non-verbal communication, in their body language, that is important for you to be attentive to and process. Listening to the other person is an important part of human connection. Who are you neglecting to truly listen to? What can you gain from giving them your undivided attention? How would that change the dynamics of your interactions and the nature of your relationship?

To show someone that you are truly listening to them and giving them your undivided attention, do the following:

1. Maintain eye contact with them.
2. Do not do anything else while you are listening.
3. Listen to details.
4. Ask questions in a nonjudgmental way.
5. Make comments that show that you have been listening.
6. Just be present and attentive.

Listening is not just an art. It is a habit that you can foster. It costs you nothing but your attention, and once you get used to it, it will become your second nature.

#83

Focus on Your Choices Rather Than on Your Circumstances

"Life is 10% what happens to you and 90% how you react to it."
—CHARLES R. SWINDOLL

Often, we feel like the victims of our life circumstances. We thought that our life would go on one path and find ourselves on a completely different path, dealing with challenges that we didn't predict, in a rapidly changing world. The biggest (and most common) mistake to make is to allow yourself to think that you are defined by your circumstances. You have no control over the circumstances. You have no control over the challenges that may come your way, good or bad. What you have complete control of is your reaction, and that reaction makes all the difference in the world. In this universe, mankind is the only living creature that has the gift of the power to choose. It is a wonderful privilege.

With anything that happens to you, no matter what it is, tell yourself:

- What happened does not define me.
- My circumstances do not define me.
- Only my actions and choices define me.
- I am powerful because I can make those choices.

Think about the different choices that you can make. Linger on your power to choose. You can write down your choices and then decide which route you would like to choose, which choice you would like to make that will define the kind of person that you are. Circumstances change. Your value remains constant—or better than that, increases over time as your skills of coping and your skills as a person in general improve, and you grow and keep growing. You are defined by your choices. Not by your circumstances.

#84

If You Want It, You've Got to Sweat for It

"Genius is one percent inspiration and
ninety-nine percent perspiration."
–Thomas Edison

When we talk about hitting the CHANGE button, we've got to talk about the value of hard work. It is the kind of hard work that takes well-defined goals and turns them into reality, step by step. Goals are the mold; hard work is what goes into the mold. Here are the five anchors of hard work that will yield fruit:

1. Hard work on aligning your focus with your goals:

We have talked about the fact that most people do not take the time to set their goals. We have also talked about how critical setting goals is for people's success. But setting goals is the easiest part of it all in terms of effort. The main challenge is in staying focused and making sure that we have done something every day, at least one thing, that brought us closer to what we are looking to accomplish. One phone call, one email, one book, one article, one completed task. Often, people are aware of their goals but their focus wanders somewhere else, and day after day passes by without making progress. Focus yourself every day by creating a simple and easy-to-follow Focus Pocus sheet: What needs to happen today so that you can take just another step toward your goals?

2. Hard work on changing your habits to habits that support your goals:

Old habits die hard, and new habits are hard work. The need to identify bad habits, pledge to change them, and then work on forming winning habits is at the heart of creating a change in your life. Ask yourself every day: Did I work on my new habits? Am I on track? What can I do tomorrow to be even more on track with my winning habits?

3. Hard work on increasing your daily productivity:

It is easy and tempting to waste time. Social media and the internet are an ongoing distraction to many. It is a lot more fun to check social media and go shopping online than to do work that will promote us, but that work requires a lot more effort and is not as entertaining. Productivity is about refocusing your attention to what really matters to you and blocking out interruptions and distractions.

4. Hard work on strategizing your next steps toward your goals:

If your goals are the GPS of your life, your strategy is the road that leads to them. Both are equally important. Take the time to strategize and break your strategy into small, daily tasks. Write them down and cross them out as you go.

5. Hard work on increasing your value:

Read more. Gain more knowledge. Improve your skills. Life is a journey of growth. Work on your growth no matter what that growth means to you. Become better at what you do. Become better in your interpersonal skills. Listen better. Communicate better. Focus more. Work on your perseverance and resilience. No matter what you do, always leave a strong impression on others, and always strive to be the best version of yourself that you can possibly be, in every aspect of your life.

#85

Dare to Dream Big

"Dare to dream, and when you dream—dream big."
—HENRIETTA SZOLD

O ne of the problem that many people face when they dare to dream big is that they'll hear from others, who would not dare to dream big, that their dream can never come true and that they need to replace it. You should dream big—you can transform your life. If it matters to you more than anything, if it matters to you so much that you don't care that you have to put in as much work as it takes, if you are willing to do what it takes, and you are willing to overcome obstacles and setbacks (and if you use the methodology of setting goals and strategizing by breaking them into smaller tasks) you can accomplish things that you never thought were possible. Wherever you think you can reach—or rather, wherever you dare to think you can reach—is where you can reach. Look at other people who do amazing things, who succeed, who live the life that they want to live. None of them became successful by dreaming small and doubting themselves. Whatever they did, and whatever choices these people made, they had one thing in common: they all dreamed big and they all believed they could do it. The best route to success is to dream big but think in terms of small daily assignments. Dreaming big is the magnet that will pull you in the desirable direction of something that inspires you, something that is important and meaningful for you, something that can completely transform your live. Thinking in terms of smaller daily tasks and shorter-term goals will ensure that you do not get overwhelmed and intimidated, that you make ongoing progress toward your goals and that you will be able to track your progress and stay on track. The people who reach the most remarkable accomplishments are often the people whom you would least expect. These may be people who do not have the resume or the track record to break the records, but they have the daring spirit to dream big, they believe that they can do it, and they are willing to put in the work and effort for it. Big goals fascinate us. They are attractive. Think of them like a magnet. The more powerful the magnet, the stronger the pull. Smaller goals have a weaker pull. In that respect, settling is an illusion of your capability and a mistake that you may very much regret later on in your life.

#86

Step by Step, Keep Going

"The journey of a thousand miles begins with one step."
—Lao Tzu

How do you eat an entire dinner? One bite at a time. Any project can be accomplished if you break it down into pieces and tackle it one piece at the time. If you have a goal that pulls you, if you have something that you are looking to accomplish that you know will transform your life to the best, the first thing to do is to look at the long-term goal, and immediately set smaller, daily and weekly tasks that will lead you to it.

The truth of the matter is that we tend to procrastinate large projects because our brains tend to focus on the enormous extent of the work ahead of us and the most difficult or challenging parts of a project, making the project seem impossible. The brain is bombarded with information to process and tends to simplify things in order to process things more quickly. This is why we classify people as "good" or "bad"—our brain basically goes through complex information and is wired to simplify it for us. The brain hates complexity. When we break a task into smaller, more digestible units, we are outsmarting our brain. Each simple task can be done. It is not as complicated and not as overwhelming to us as the bigger dream, goal, or target accomplishment may be. In focusing on smaller tasks, one thing at a time, and making progress in simple yet steady steps, we have outsmarted our brain and prevented it from getting overwhelmed, which would cause us to avoid or procrastinate and reject the challenge. Step by step, big wins. Outsmart your brain toward your goal.

#87

Position Yourself as a Leader

*"Whenever you find yourself on
the side of the majority, it is
time to pause and reflect."*
—MARK TWAIN

Positioning yourself as a leader means that you choose to get off the beaten path that everyone else around you is on. You don't do what everyone does, you don't dream what everyone dreams, you don't make the same choices that they make, and you don't compare yourself to them. You don't listen to other people's justifications when you know that these are excuses to choices that will not promote you. You keep on going when they quit. You get on a different path. You can choose your own role models for that path and learn from them, but you end up doing your own thing. You model, with your own choices, how to do things differently and how great the gain is. In the way you manage your choices, you become a role model and an inspiration to others. You set the highest standards for yourself in whatever you do. You accept full responsibility when you mess up. You strategize your choices and you do not act impulsively and then regret it. You avoid doing more of the same. You are open to new things and you challenge yourself every day. That's leadership.

People do not become leaders because they decide to be leaders. People become leaders because they challenge themselves in ways that other people do not. They become leaders when they stop making excuses.

Position yourself as a leader by challenging yourself toward your biggest dreams. You will surely become an inspiration to others. Your choices will give them the courage to challenge themselves and the circumstances that they encounter.

#88

Work with What You've Got

"Victory belongs to the most persevering."
—NAPOLEON BONAPARTE

Lamenting the resources that you do not have in order to accomplish your goals, the money that you need, the education that you need, the support that you need in order for your goal to be accomplished, quickly becomes no more than an excuse for not going for it. Yes, having certain resources accessible to you surely makes things easier in some respects, but since that is not what you are working with, you will need to win with the resources that you do have. Avoid putting your focus on what your goal takes that you do not have, and focus on the resources that you do have. As meager as they may seem to you, achieving your goal depends more on your power of will than on resources. We all know the famous biblical David and Goliath story where David won the battle in spite of his meager resources, as he was nothing but a shepherd boy with a stone in his hand. It is not the power of resources that will make it or break it for you. It is the power of passion, purpose and daring.

#89

Rise Up from Rock Bottom

"Success is how high you bounce when you hit bottom."
—GEORGE S. PATTON

We have talked about the fact that setbacks are to be expected along the road to accomplishing your goals and achieving the life that you want. What then happens when you feel that you hit rock bottom? When you feel that you are so close to despair that you do not know where to continue and how to pull yourself up? Remember this, many of the most successful people hit rock bottom at least once along the way. If that happens to you, think of all of these extremely successful people that were once in your place. If you hit rock bottom, you take a deep breath, and you start planning your comeback. Remember, you only have control over three things in your life: your thoughts, your actions, and your reactions. While this may not seem like much, it is actually a lot more than you realize. These three things, your thoughts, actions, and reactions, give you a tremendous amount of power to determine what happens next. If you choose to focus on pain and suffering, you will have very limited progress. However, if you choose to focus your thoughts on bouncing back, you will bounce back even higher and your comeback will then become stronger than your setback. You will restore your passion. You will restore your purpose, and you will restore your sense of ownership in taking charge of your own life. Root for yourself. Plan your next win. A setback is just a setback, and from rock bottom you can only go up.

#90

Take Charge of Your Future

"We are made wise not by the recollection of the past, but by the responsibility for our future."
—George Bernard Shaw

Moving away from a painful past is not a simple task, but not doing so is detrimental for taking your future into your hands. Many of us have haunting memories in our past—traumas that we went through, loved ones that we have lost, things that we regret and things that are painful for us. Holding onto pain is normal, and it is normal for us to take the time to process and to try to make sense of it in our mind. But it is also normal to let go and move forward after an appropriate period of time. The first step to take is be totally honest with yourself and decide if you are ready to move forward. Yes, you went through something difficult that made your life different and more challenging, but you have the power to choose here, and your choice will shape your future. You do not have to live in a victim state of mind. You can make a different choice and decide to put in the mental work that is needed for it. Take the time to imagine to yourself what your life would look like after moving forward and away from your past. Imagine your healing. You will not be erasing your painful memories. They are a part of your life now, whether you want them or not. But you can make the choice to put them in your mind in a place that will allow you to continue forward and design the life that you choose for yourself.

#91

Just push through

*"No matter the circumstances that you may be
going through, just push through it."*
–RAY LEWIS

One of the most challenging parts of your journey toward your goals
or making a lasting change in your life is when you are pushing
through difficulty. Many people give up at this phase, because obstacles
create many challenging feelings for them. If you got a rejection letter
from an employer, your ego may be hurt. If you quit your job to pursue
the career of your dreams, your sense of security may be compromised.
Sometimes the most difficult obstacle to overcome is the tempting will to
give up, the inner self voice that tells you that you will not succeed and
that you need to give up. Here are the four best strategies for pushing
through difficulty:

1. Identify the challenge by name, and set up your mind to deal
   with it.
2. Identify and accept your emotions about the situation, and
   then decide to push through anyway.
3. Celebrate all milestones, as small as they may be, and give
   yourself credit for conquering them.
4. Argue with your inner voice that tells you that you cannot do
   something. Ask your inner voice: Who put that thought in
   my mind that I cannot do it? Why wouldn't I be able to do it?

#92

Stop Standing in Your Own Way

"If you find a path with no obstacles, it probably doesn't lead anywhere."
—Frank A. Clark

In order to have breakthroughs in your life, you need to stop setting yourself up for failure. Many of us tend to exhibit habits that set us up for failure, without even realizing that what we are doing is working against us. Here are the three most common ways of standing in your own way and setting yourself up for failures. See if you recognize yourself in any of these, and take control now so that you stop setting yourself up and start making steps toward the life that you want:

1. Procrastination:

Many people use procrastination as a subconscious defense mechanism, because it provides the perfect excuse for setting yourself up for failure. This is where you tell yourself: "If only I had enough time to get this right/to study for the test/to prepare for the meeting, I definitely would have nailed it." We all have 24 hours a day. You were not prepared because you didn't manage your time well.

2. Too busy:

Being too busy is not a form of success. Being too busy means that you don't know how to prioritize and you don't know when to say no and what to say no to. Do not overextend yourself. To win this, you need to learn to say no and you need to prioritize.

3. No short-term goals:

Having long-term goals is where you start, but if you do not have short-term goals broken into daily tasks, time will go by and you will keep dreaming. Take your dream and turn it into a plan, and follow up on it daily and weekly.

#93

Turn your challenges into your engine

"Turn your wounds into wisdom."
—Oprah

The difference between people in terms of the impact that challenges have on their lives is in the way they respond to them. When challenges come along, no matter what they are, it is in your hands to either let them discourage you, or let them fuel your motivation even more. You can feel the burn of your determination to do what you need to do, get to where you want to get in life, in spite of your challenges, and decide that they do not define you, and that you are going to face them.

Here are three ways to turn your challenge into your fuel:

1. Use the disbelievers as your fuel.

There will always be those disbelievers who cast doubt on new business, new change, new challenges, and anything new and daring that you are trying to aim for in your life. That is who you do *not* want to be. That doubtful mindset is what you are stepping away from. Use their doubt as fuel.

2. Remember that necessity is the mother of resourcefulness.

When something happens that forces you to step up your game, it may seem at first like a difficult hardship or setback. Remember this: Necessity creates urgency. Urgency leads to resourcefulness. That difficulty will make you better. It is your blessing in disguise.

Ultimately, this will lead to a pivot in your life or a real breakthrough.

3. Harness everything that comes your way as a learning experience.

Any challenge in life, in business, or in any aspect of your being can be viewed as a learning experience. Take a look at what happened and see what lessons can be applied from it. Is there a way to learn from it and do things differently going forward?

#94

Make it about Something Bigger Than Yourself

"People do not decide to become extraordinary. They decide to accomplish extraordinary things."
—EDMUND HILLARY

There are three levels of goals that we set for ourselves: individual, familial, and spiritual.

1. Individual Goals:

Our individual goals are the most basic goals. This is where our main focus is: increasing our standard of living, making more money, or upgrading our home. On this level, we act for the pleasure of our own ego.

2. Familial Goals:

Goals on a familial level include a motivation to do more for the people we love. These would be things like setting an example for our children, giving them a better education and opportunities, or providing the family with a more comfortable life.

3. Spiritual Goals:

Goals on a spiritual level are set when we feel connected to something larger than ourselves, when we are driven to our highest level of achievement and challenge ourselves to do something that will leave a legacy and outlive our existence.

With each level of your goals, from individual to family to spiritual, you become more resilient. The higher purpose gives you the power to overcome whatever comes your way. It is completely ok and a wonderful thing to have individual goals, and most people start with that, but the more your goal is connected to people and ideas that are beyond your ego, the less shaky you are on your path and the more resilient you become against all odds and circumstances.

#95

You Always Have More Options
Than You Realize

"Be miserable, or motivate yourself. Whatever
has to be done, it's always your choice."
–WAYNE DYER

People often get very frustrated because they see very limited options to solve the problems that they are facing. We call that phenomena Tunnel Vision. **Tunnel vision** describes the limited ability to consider alternatives to our preferred line of thought. This is where our mind is preconditioned to a certain solution or outcome. This is why a second opinion, or brainstorming within a team, is so critical. In engaging more than one mind in solving a problem, a challenge, or a situation, we are getting more than one mind to look at the situation from additional perspectives, without the same biases and preconceptions. One of the main demotivating things to happen to anyone is when people cannot see more than one or two ways to solve a problem, and none work for them. The ability to join forces with others, to realize that we have more options that we did not even consider, is empowering and liberating, and carves the way to move forward rather than staying stuck.

If you feel stuck, and feel like you only have one or two options, do not despair. Do this instead:

Reach out to others to brainstorm solutions.

Talk to other people about the problem without expecting solutions—solutions will come to your mind as you are talking about it.

Look for ways to get inspired. Listen to clips, watch something inspiring, read an inspiring book. Inspiration will empower you to open your mind to new ideas.

#96

Hold Yourself Accountable
Every Step of the Way

"It is not in the stars to hold our destiny but in ourselves."
—WILLIAM SHAKESPEARE

Breaking habits is hard, and starting new ones can be even harder. When you're on the strenuous and adventurous path of success and determination, shedding old habits and creating new ones is a necessary part of the journey.

A lot of people struggle with accomplishing their goals, usually because they don't have enough time to complete the task at hand, and instead of completing it, they stress about not having the time to complete it.

It's a vicious cycle, but you absolutely have the power to stop it.

Think about it: When you continue to make goals and not reach them, you create that habit. You create a story in your mind that tells you that when you start something, you probably won't finish it. Before you've even embarked on the journey, your mind has started to sabotage your progress with doubts.

Keeping up with your goals trains your mind to continue doing exactly that—set goals and meet them, set more goals and meet them too. By then, that pattern becomes both a part of your narrative about yourself and a habit.

On the other end, when you let yourself miss opportunities to reach your goals, you start to lose your belief in your ability, and that becomes a self-sabotaging narrative in your head, where you tell yourself that you are just not able to follow through.

Start checking off your daily tasks toward your goals. This one habit will become a positive reinforcement for a positive self-narrative and a habit of making things happen.

#97

Hold Yourself to the Highest Standards

*"Hold yourself responsible to a higher
standard than anyone expects of
you. Never excuse yourself."*
–Henry Ward Beecher

Your life is shaped by the decisions that you make. Each day, you make many decisions for yourself. These decisions can promote you or become a complete waste of time, money, and energy. One way to ensure you are making the most progress possible on your journey to success is to hold yourself to a higher standard.

Successful people, and for that purpose the definition is, people who have managed to transform their lives and take their destiny into their hands one way or another, have stayed motivated and put in the hard work necessary to make a name for themselves. They never took the easy way out or cut corners when they had the chance.

If you are surrounded by people who do not set the highest standards for themselves, view yourself on a different level and make it your responsibility to become a role model in the way you carry yourself and conduct your life. If you feel that the people around you have a negative influence on your attitude and state of mind, take a step or two back. It is easy to be like everyone else, to simply follow the path everyone follows every day. It is one of the simplest things to do. This is where we simply go through life every day, expecting and wishing that things were much better, always hoping for a better way while we sometimes have all it takes to be what we want to be. We just think it is not enough and hope we can get something better. With what we have, we can be what we want to be.

Make yourself better every day. Hold yourself to the highest standards.

#98

Keep Yourself Challenged

"The two enemies of human happiness are pain and boredom."
—ARTHUR SCHOPENHAUER

K eeping yourself challenged stands in complete opposition to what
we inherently tend to be geared toward: keeping ourselves safe and
comfortable. Unfortunately, safe and comfortable keep you exactly where
you are at, and put you at risk anyway. There is no safe, and comfortable
is only temporary. Not only that, you will not tap into even a fraction
of your potential that way. You are also putting yourself at risk. This is a
rapidly changing world. You cannot just sit still and hope for comfortable.
It simply will not work in the long term. Try to always have something
going that stretches your limits. This could be learning a new skill or
trying something new. It will let you stretch the muscles of your capability
and will get you out of the autopilot mode of doing more of the same
over and over again. You can start with smaller challenges and work your
way up. Over time, challenge yourself more. The more success happens
to you after you have challenged yourself, the more confident you will
become in your ability to go for it again. Challenge doesn't just help you
grow your skills. It helps you grow your being.

#99

Create Your Own Opportunities

"To hell with circumstances; I create opportunities."
—BRUCE LEE

You attract and create your own opportunities by becoming better than you currently are. You do this by becoming more disciplined, more skilled both professionally and in terms of interpersonal skills. You create more opportunities by becoming more creative to see what's out there and shape and use it for your own advantage. You need to become more creative in the approach you take, in the attitude you have, in the way you see things. This takes courage. You need courage to see things differently. You need courage to get off the beaten path and not do what everyone else does, think what everyone else thinks, have the same mental attitude that other people have around you. You need to become more courageous in choosing to take action. You need to become better at seeing the future in the present. To take advantage of an unfortunate situation rather than be burdened by it. It is in your hands. You need to be more hard working and look for opportunities. They will not come to you like a package at your door. You need to seek them, think creatively, find a way to keep your mind open and your thoughts sharp and positive. Creating opportunities is the ultimate form of taking your life into your hands. It is the ultimate form of accountability. Having that state of mind is a matter of choice. A life-transforming choice in every possible way.

#100

Hold the Wheel, You Are in Control of Your Life!

"The best years of your life are the ones in which you decide your problems are your own. You do not blame them on your mother, the ecology or the president. You realize that you control your own destiny."
—ALBERT ELLIS

The realization that you are in control of your destiny, that you are in control of your reality, is alarming at first. We are so used to blaming our circumstances—our childhood, our opportunities, our parents, our spouses or ex-spouses, our boss—and living within an imaginary circle that we have drawn around ourselves. Change in our lives is possible only if we change our state of mind and understand that our attitude is the basis for everything that transpires in our lives. This book was written not only for advice but also for encouragement. It is remarkable to see everyday people doing remarkable things within extremely challenging situations. We all have that within us, we just sometimes don't realize the power of a winning attitude to create successful and lasting changes that we crave to see in our lives. Read this book when you feel discouraged. Read this book when things get challenging and you need to remind yourself that—with a well-defined, workable plan and determination—you can do anything that you set your mind to do. You can overcome hardship and reach new destinations in your life that you never thought were even an option for you. You can do amazing things, transforming your life and the lives of those who matter to you the most. It is all in your hands.